THE PERSECUTION OF SARAH PALIN

ALSO BY MATTHEW CONTINETTI

The K Street Gang: The Rise and Fall of the Republican Machine

THE PERSECUTION

of

SARAH PALIN

How the Elite Media Tried to Bring Down a Rising Star

MATTHEW CONTINETTI

Sentinel

SENTINEL

Published by the Penguin Group

Penguin Group (USA) Inc., 375 Hudson Street,
New York, New York 10014, U.S.A.
Penguin Group (Canada), 90 Eglinton Avenue East, Suite 700,
Toronto, Ontario, Canada M4P 2Y3
(a division of Pearson Penguin Canada Inc.)
Penguin Books Ltd, 80 Strand, London WC2R 0RL, England
Penguin Ireland, 25 St. Stephen's Green, Dublin 2, Ireland
(a division of Penguin Books Ltd)
Penguin Books Australia Ltd, 250 Camberwell Road, Camberwell,
Victoria 3124, Australia
(a division of Pearson Australia Group Pty Ltd)
Penguin Books India Pvt Ltd, 11 Community Centre, Panchsheel Park,
New Delhi – 110 017, India
Penguin Group (NZ), 67 Apollo Drive, Rosedale, North Shore 0632,
New Zealand (a division of Pearson New Zealand Ltd)
Penguin Books (South Africa) (Pty) Ltd, 24 Sturdee Avenue,
Rosebank, Johannesburg 2196, South Africa

Penguin Books Ltd, Registered Offices:
80 Strand, London WC2R 0RL, England

First published in 2009 by Sentinel,
a member of Penguin Group (USA) Inc.

1   3   5   7   9   10   8   6   4   2

LIBRARY OF CONGRESS CATALOGING IN PUBLICATION DATA

Continetti, Matthew.
    The persecution of Sarah Palin : how the elite media tried to bring down a rising star / by Matthew Continetti.
      p. cm.
    ISBN 978-1-59523-061-4
    1. Palin, Sarah, 1964—In mass media.   2. Journalism—Objectivity—United States.   3. Mass media—Objectivity—United
States.   4. Political campaigns—United States—Press coverage—United States.   5. Press and politics—United States.
6. Presidents—United States—Election—2008.   I. Title.
    F910.7.P35C665 2009
    979.8'052092—dc22   2009039426

Printed in the United States of America
Set in Adobe Garamond
Designed by Spring Hoteling

TO MY BROTHER

"What the new journalism seeks is what once upon a time was called 'sensationalism,' though no one in today's media would permit that term to be used. It wants scandal, it wants heated controversy, it wants excitement, it wants titillation, above all it lusts for human sacrifices and the destruction of reputations."

—IRVING KRISTOL

Contents

THE PERSECUTION OF SARAH PALIN

PROLOGUE
The Palin Myth: From Hero to Harpy in Eight Short Weeks

ONE morning in the fall of 2008, Sarah Palin awoke to discover that she had been changed into a monster.

This was no Kafka story, however. As recently as late August of that year, Palin had been an extremely popular governor of Alaska, known to her constituents as a bipartisan reformer who championed clean government. Now, as John McCain's running mate, the world knew her instead as a heat-packing, moose-eating, wolf-hunting, makeup-wearing, idiotic, apocalyptic harpy. She had become a freak.

If you listened to Democrats and the mainstream media, you learned that Palin was a Buchananite (she wasn't), a member of the Alaskan Independence Party (nope), and a biblical literalist who believed dinosaurs roamed the earth several thousand years ago (an utter fabrication); that she was anticontraception (incorrect), wanted to teach creationism in schools (not really), and didn't believe that man may be contributing to global warming (untrue); that she banned books (a gross distortion), claimed she could see Russia from her house (never happened), faked her pregnancy (unbelievable), slept with her husband's business associate (a myth), thought the Iraq war was a mission from God (not so), and didn't know that Africa was a continent (baloney).

When they weren't mangling facts, the press did their best to undermine Palin's accomplishments. Reputable news outlets reported that she hadn't really sold her predecessor's jet, didn't actually stop the Bridge to Nowhere, inflated the importance of the natural gas pipeline she had championed, cut funding for teenage moms and children with special needs, and never gave a press conference during the presidential campaign. This was all hokum.

The Project for Excellence in Journalism found that Sarah Palin received much more negative coverage than she did positive. Those writers and communicators who were unconstrained by pretensions to objectivity went even further. Feminist activists denied Palin her womanhood because she did not share their politics. Comedians made fun of her accent, clothes, smarts, and looks. The same campaign operatives who had recommended Palin to John McCain turned on her, telling reporters (on background, of course) that Palin was an incompetent "diva," a "hillbilly" who may have been suffering from postpartum depression.

Palin was routinely insulted and described in the crudest language. She has been called a "freak show," a "joke," an "extreme liability," a "turncoat b*tch," an "insult," a "fire-breather," "xenophobic," a "sitcom of a vice-presidential choice," a "disaster movie," a "shallow" person, "chirpy," a "provincial," a "disgrace to women" who was "as fake as they come," a "nauseating," "cocky wacko," a "jack in the box," "Napoleon in bunny boots," "extreme," "radical," a "vessel," a "farce," "Bush in drag," "not very bright," "utterly unqualified," a "bimbo," "Danielle Quayle," the "new spokesperson for bellicosity and confrontation," a "fatal cancer," "like a really bad Disney movie," "laughable," an "odd combination of Chauncey Gardiner from *Being There* and Marge from *Fargo*," "dangerous," a "bully," the "biggest demagogue in America," the "Paleolithic Princess of Parsimonious Patriotism," the "anti–Wonder Woman," "judgmental," "dictatorial" with a "superior religious self-righteousness," a "racist" who was "absurd," "scary," and a "token," a "bantamweight cheerleader," an "airhead," an "idiot," a "librarian in a porn film," a "Jesus freak," a "man with a vagina," a "big reactionary," a "maniac," a "whore," a "two-bit caricature culled from some cutting-room-floor episode of *Roseanne*," a "symbol of everything that is wrong with the modern United States," the "tawdriest, most half-a**ed fraud imaginable," a "character too dumb even for daytime TV," a "puffed-up dimwit with primitive religious beliefs," "totally nuts," "bonkers," an "ex-beauty queen governor on the job only twenty months, fanatically antiabortion and pro-gun," "much worse than ridiculous," "insulting," a "train wreck," an "incompetent," a "snarling b*tch," a "compulsive, repetitive, demonstrable liar," an "[expletive deleted] psychopath," a "religious fanatic and a proud, boastful ignoramus," "political slime," a "mean, brain-dead rat," a "bad mother" who "often seems proud of what she does not know," the "Carmela Soprano of the GOP," a "Drama Queen," a "Republican blow-up doll" who "ideologically" is "their hardcore pornographic centerfold spread," an "opportunistic antifemale," a "true Stepford candidate, a cyborg," a "quitter," and—this list is by no means exhaustive—a "bonbon."

The reaction to Sarah Palin was visceral, nasty, and unrelenting. "Our state was inundated with opposition researchers trying to dig up dirt, the Democratic blogosphere up here making stuff up," Palin told me during an interview for the *Weekly Standard* in July 2009. Widespread ignorance about her biography and accomplishments did not prevent the pundits from declaring that they knew precisely what Palin was all about. The response to her presence was not intellectual; it was emotional. When

Palin arrived on the national scene, the people who loved her did not have enough information on which to base their love, and the people who hated her did not have the information on which to base their hatred. Something else, something psychological, was going on.

Sarah Palin could not be more unlike her public caricature. When she became John McCain's running mate, she was neither a party-line Republican nor a movement conservative. She is an unpredictable and courageous politician who has the ability to identify situations where the public is out of sync with the establishment, from conservatives tired of nonpartisan municipal management in Wasilla, Alaska, to Alaskans angry at corruption and apathy in Juneau, to—potentially—Americans upset at the Obama Democrats' big-spending, over-regulating agenda.

Throughout her professional life, Sarah Palin has challenged the dominant power structure and overturned the accepted, elite narrative of the way things ought to be. Her town establishment said that Wasilla is a place where a sales tax will solve everyone's problems, and partisan and ideological politics do not matter. Palin argued otherwise. Her state establishment declared that Juneau ought to be run by a cozy network of Republican lawmakers and energy interests. Palin didn't think so. The media establishment decreed that Barack Obama was going to rescue the country from eight years of George W. Bush. Palin threw a wrench into Obama's plans.

The left has tried to bar Sarah Palin from running for higher office and seeks to delegitimize her. When Palin became a national figure, she also became a threat to liberal aspirations. Here was a young, attractive, and pro-life conservative mom who connected with ordinary Americans. What the left did in response was launch a campaign of distortion, exaggeration, fabrication, vilification, ridicule, and abuse. Here is how senior Democrats greeted Sarah Palin's nomination, according to Monica Langley in the November 5, 2008, *Wall Street Journal:*

The Obama campaign watched her rousing performance at the Republican convention and focus groups assembled to test the voter reaction. Obama advisers couldn't believe what they were hearing. "Sarah Palin is one of us" was an oft-heard refrain. "She can help John McCain shake up Washington" was another common theme.

On his weekly strategy call with Democratic senators after the Republican convention in early September, Obama Chief of Staff Jim Messina began, "Let me walk you through this week's events." He was cut off by angry senators calling for a more aggressive response to the Republican running-mate pick: "Go after Palin." "Define Palin." "Make the race about Palin." Mr. Messina was startled by the new nervousness in the party ranks.

And so began the persecution of Sarah Louise Palin.

The Feral Beast

Resistance to Palin has always been fierce. At every stage in her career, she has been belittled and underestimated. The critics have said that she doesn't have enough experience, that she misses the finer points of policy, that she runs haphazard campaigns. And yet more often than not Palin has won. She has crushed her opponents. An Anchorage businessman, no fan of Palin, said it well: "Sarah is a great warrior," he told me.

There was a time when the media appreciated Palin's political skill. The October 15, 2007, edition of *Newsweek* contained an article about two up-and-coming Western governors: Democrat Janet Napolitano of Arizona and Republican Sarah Palin of Alaska. "[G]overnors like Napolitano, 49, and Palin, 43, are making their mark with a pragmatic, postpartisan approach to solving problems," Karen Breslau wrote, "a style that works especially well with the large numbers of independent voters in their respective states."

Breslau briefly profiled both women. "In Alaska," she wrote, "Palin is challenging the dominant, sometimes corrupting, role of oil companies in the state's political culture . . . Although she has been in office less than a year, Palin, too, earns high marks from lawmakers on the other side of the aisle." What makes the article striking is its positive tone. It was one of the few times Sarah Palin ever received balanced and net-favorable coverage in the mainstream media.

By September 2008, however, the atmosphere surrounding Palin was quite different. "Alaska's young governor is as riven with contradictions and complexities as the state itself," the *Newsweek* staff wrote in the magazine's September 15, 2008, issue, in an article to which Karen Breslau contributed reporting. "A devoted mother, Palin is now running for national office, exposing her young family to the warping effects of international scrutiny. A reformer, she faces allegations of exerting improper influence in city and state government. A self-styled regular Red State gal, she is relentlessly driven, a politician of epic ambition who is running against a Washington establishment that, if elected, she will inevitably join, and even rule over. "

Yet *Newsweek* was identifying contradictions that did not actually exist.

On September 22, the feminist author Naomi Wolf posted a paranoid and malicious screed on the *Huffington Post* that was typical of the way left-wing writers talked about Sarah Palin after she secured the Republican vice presidential nomination. "I believe the Rove-Cheney cabal is using Sarah Palin as a stalking horse, an Evita figure, to put a popular, populist face on the coming police state and be the talk show hostess for the end of elections as we know them," Wolf wrote. "If McCain-Palin get in, this will be the last true American election. She will be working for Halliburton, KBR, Rove and Cheney into the fore-seeable future—for a decade perhaps—a puppet 'president' for the same people who have plundered our treasure, are now holding the US econ-omy hostage and who murdered four thousand brave young men and women in a way [*sic*] of choice and lies. . . . Under the coming Palin-Rove police state, you will witness the plans now under way to bring Iraqi troops to patrol the streets of our nation."

How did Palin metamorphose from being the poster girl for "a pragmatic, postpartisan approach" to being the "popular, populist face on the coming police state"? The answer has partly to do with culture and partly to do with technology. If you had gone into a chemical laboratory to concoct a politician whose background and manner would sound liberal alarms, you probably would have come up with someone like Sarah Palin. For this reason, the response to Palin was similar to the reaction liberals had to George W. Bush. The left recoils at a certain swagger, a manner of speech, and a lack of cultural embar-rassment that the two share. Neither Bush nor Palin mind the fact that they are not part of this country's cognoscenti. But until Palin showed up, one could have written off the liberal reaction to Bush as simply anti-Texan bias. That wasn't it, however. Palin proved that at its root the reaction to these folksy Western politicians is a form of antiprovincial-ism; a distaste for those who hail from outside America's coastal me-tropolises; a revulsion toward people who do not aspire to adopt the norms, values, politics, and attitudes of the Eastern cultural elite.

Over the course of the Bush presidency, American liberals con-structed a vast and complicated machinery of demonization and hatred. Democratic politicians, progressive think tanks, and liberal blogs did all they could to portray Republicans, Bush in particular, as dangerous, extreme, ignorant, dishonest, and corrupt. The mainstream media be-came more partisan and embittered and recklessly exposed national security secrets on their front pages and nightly newscasts. The Internet, a medium that specializes in fomenting primitive rumor and venomous group-think, sensationalized facts, tarred reputations, and allowed disgruntled liberals to contrive conspiracies and vent absurdities for the sole purpose of bringing Bush and the conservatives to heel. The mainstream media took their cues from the partisan and vitriolic blogosphere. As Tony Blair put it in a June 12, 2007, speech at the Reuters headquarters in London, "Today's media, more than ever before, hunts in a pack. In these modes it is like a feral beast, just tearing people and reputations to bits. But no one dares miss out."

The beast indisputably took sides in the 2008 election. Let Oprah tell it: "He is The One!" she cried in December 2007. "He is The One! . . . Barack Obama!" On MSNBC's *Hardball with Chris Matthews* in the summer of 2009, *Newsweek* writer Evan Thomas likened Obama to God. The media clearly favored Obama over Hillary Clinton in the Democratic primary and over John McCain in the general election. Obama is their guy. And when the beast saw Sarah Palin appear out of thin air and captivate the American imagination, it tore her apart. The hate machine whirred and hummed and swung into high gear.

Lies became facts, the smarmiest allegations jumped to Page One, and anybody who had something horrible to say about Sarah Palin was handed a megaphone and told to speak as loudly as possible. Wherever the Palin-haters gathered, they flaunted their contempt. Anything that complicated their prearranged story was shunted aside. Bias, inaccuracy, and self-obsession ruled the day. The pack became frenzied. Rabid. They did not miss a single opportunity to slight Palin. They could not leave her alone—even after the election was over and their preferred candidate had won; even after Palin resigned her office in July 2009.

This is a book about how the feral beast hunted down its prey.

And how she fought back.

CHAPTER ONE
The Golden Ticket: When John Met Sarah

HE'D beaten the odds. He'd won, and the prize was his. Finally.

The night of March 4, 2008, John McCain won four Republican presidential primaries: Texas, Ohio, Vermont, and Rhode Island. The race for the 2008 GOP presidential nomination was over. Former Arkansas governor Mike Huckabee bid farewell to the campaign trail that night, pledging his support to the Arizona senator. McCain's other major rival for the nomination, former Massachusetts governor Mitt Romney, had left the race a month earlier. Only the renegade Republican congressman Ron Paul stayed in contention. But Paul did not win a single state (though he did finish second in ten states), so there was no actual possibility of his becoming the party's nominee. The job was McCain's.

McCain had wanted this chance for a long time. He had been on Bob Dole's vice presidential shortlist in 1996 but was passed over in favor of Jack Kemp. McCain's first attempt at the top job came in 2000, when his whopping upset victory over front-runner George W. Bush in the New Hampshire primary shocked the Republican establishment and injected excitement into what had been a dull race. Still, Bush won both his party's nomination and the presidency (though just barely).

That was not the end of the story, however. McCain became one of the forty-third president's strongest critics from 2001 to 2004. He opposed almost all of Bush's major domestic policy initiatives, including the 2001 and 2003 tax cuts and the 2003 Medicare prescription drug bill. This period saw Bush and McCain at loggerheads over drilling in the Arctic National Wildlife Refuge, ethanol subsidies, the inquiry into the 9/11 terrorist attacks, campaign finance reform, troop levels in Iraq, and terrorist detention and interrogation policy. The disputes became so pronounced that the 2004 Democratic presidential nominee, Massachusetts senator John Kerry, asked McCain to join *his* ticket as vice president. McCain demurred. He opted for a rapprochement with Bush, strongly campaigning for the president's reelection and delivering one of the most effective speeches at the 2004 GOP convention.

McCain hewed more closely to the president's second-term agenda. He supported the nominations of John Roberts and Samuel Alito to the Supreme Court in 2005 and 2006, respectively, backed the failed Bush immigration reform bills in 2006 and 2007, and became the most vocal supporter of Bush's 2007 surge of troops into Iraq. McCain was still willing to take on his own party—he led the inquiry into the Jack Abramoff lobbying scandals that helped bring down House majority leader Tom DeLay—but his criticism was less pronounced. Where he differed with the president on issues like climate change legislation, interrogation methods, and spending, McCain let his position be known, but he did not lead the opposition against the White House. He was more interested in repairing his relationships with GOP powerbrokers. He was more interested in running for president in 2008.

At the Conservative Political Action Conference (CPAC) in 2007, I was surprised to hear activists boo lustily whenever they heard McCain's name. But I had forgotten just how much conservative activists disliked the Arizona senator for his policy apostasy, his attacks on leaders of the religious right such as Jerry Falwell and Pat Robertson, and his favorable media coverage—even if that coverage would not stay favorable for long. McCain started his run for president in 2007 as the presumed front-runner but soon found himself floundering. All his efforts to patch things up with the GOP base didn't seem to be working. His support for immigration reform that effectively amnestied millions of illegal immigrants put him squarely at odds with most Republicans. Throughout the summer of 2007, McCain's poll numbers sank like a stone.

Then McCain made a fateful decision. He ignored the advisers who were telling him to back off from supporting Bush and the surge. He doubled-down. He made the Iraq war his signature issue. It was the first real gamble of his campaign, and it paid off. The summer of 2007 was bloody in Iraq, but during the fall, McCain argued persuasively that the counterinsurgency campaign was working. American casualties began to decline. Voters trusted the American commander in Iraq, General David Petraeus, and they identified McCain with the general's steady bearing and successful prosecution of the war.

McCain was no slouch when it came to national security and world affairs. The former navy pilot and POW was a genuine American hero. When he told the audience at an October 2007 GOP debate that he hadn't attended the "cultural and pharmaceutical event" Woodstock because "I was tied up at the time," the crowd leaped to its feet, applauding and cheering. That was the moment when McCain established a gut connection with much of the GOP electorate. They admired his military service. They trusted his judgment.

The GOP field's weaknesses helped him, too. All the major candidates for the nomination had liabilities. McCain wasn't conservative enough. Romney had flipped to the pro-life position only recently, his signature issue in Massachusetts had been an expensive universal health insurance mandate, and his Mormon faith was suspect to many Christians. Former New York City mayor Rudy Giuliani was tough on terrorism and aggressively pro-business, but he was also pro-choice, thrice married, and had long supported gun control. The long shot Huckabee was an excellent communicator and a legitimate social conservative, but his populism scared off the Republican moneybags who fund campaigns. Former Tennessee senator Fred Thompson was a Southern conservative who passed every litmus test, but he did not seem very interested in campaigning.

When the primaries began, Huckabee and Romney split the conservative vote and thereby ceded the moderates (and the nomination) to McCain. Huckabee took Iowa and most of the Deep South. Romney's self-financing allowed him to organize and win states where delegates were allotted through party caucuses, where he had strong personal connections, and where there was a large Mormon population; that gave him a total of eleven states. Giuliani flamed out entirely, betting his entire candidacy on the relatively late Florida primary, where he came in third. McCain won the two most important early primary states, New Hampshire and South Carolina, but with less than 40 percent of the vote in each—not exactly a ringing endorsement, but still enough for victory.

The GOP emerged from its presidential primary in a unique position. In a year when by all reasonable measures—incumbent presidential job approval, fund-raising totals, and party identification—the Republican ticket was destined to lose, the party had somehow nominated the one man who could conceivably win. McCain was a widely respected figure. Independents admired him. His positions on climate change, immigration, counterterrorism, and ethics in government all jibed with the public mood. And his experience in Washington and abroad trumped that of the likely Democratic nominee, Senator Barack Obama.

McCain is superstitious. He did not want to seriously contemplate his vice presidential selection until he knew the nomination was his. It wasn't until sometime after the Texas primary that he asked his friend Arthur B. Culvahouse, a partner at the international law firm O'Melveny & Myers, to begin examining the likely prospects. The decision was fast approaching. The veepstakes had begun.

THE SECOND FRONT

Why did John McCain choose Sarah Palin as his vice presidential nominee? The choice cannot be separated from its historical moment. By the end of the summer, McCain had pulled within a few points of Obama. He had settled on the message that Obama was a frivolous celebrity who could not be trusted with governing the country. He had found an issue in domestic drilling for energy. He was a unique messenger who appealed to the center and could speak frankly about the problems his copartisan George W. Bush had been unable to solve.

A few things still were missing, however. One was that McCain suffered from an enthusiasm gap. His supporters were nowhere near as excited about the election as Obama's were. Furthermore, the incumbent president's legacy did not bolster conservative passion. Bush had launched the country into a long, unpopular war that America had only recently begun to win. He had presided over a record spike in gasoline prices at the same time that median incomes failed to increase appreciably. He had allowed Republican Congresses to spend profligately. The country more or less had tuned him out after the Katrina debacle. Why on earth would they replace him with a member of the same party?

Perhaps the only way for McCain to pull off an upset, then, would have been for him to persuade Americans that the Democratic candidate was too risky. But that was difficult in a political environment where the media treated Obama as the second coming and run-of-the-mill conservatives felt no real affection for the GOP nominee. McCain was powerless in the face of the media slant toward Obama, but he could choose a vice presidential nominee with an eye toward his base. Hardly anyone in the Lower 48 knew who Sarah Palin was, but she was more likely to excite conservatives than, say, Minnesota governor Tim Pawlenty.

The other missing element was a sense that a President McCain would be a true change from President Bush. Obama had used the "change" theme expertly. He and his advisers had predicted early on that the Democratic primary electorate and the overall U.S. public were looking for something different than what they'd experienced over the last eight years. Obama deployed the specter of change to sink Hillary Clinton, and now he was deploying the same message to sink McCain. McCain's response to the "change" message had been Clinton's: experience is more important.

A lack of experience does not disqualify presidential candidates, however. Again and again, voters have elected inexperienced outsiders: Jimmy Carter, Bill Clinton, George W. Bush (and, in November 2008, Barack Obama). McCain and his team watched as Hillary Clinton's "experience" message failed. What would happen, though, if McCain also ran on a change platform? What if he opened a second front, running just as much against the incumbent Republican Party as the Obama insurrection?

In order for McCain to run on his own change message, he needed a running mate who had no ties to the Washington Republicans. Someone unassociated with the Bush GOP. Someone with a record of challenging power networks, both Democratic and Republican. Someone who might be able to draw off the female independent voters who were upset that Hillary Clinton had been denied the Democratic nomination. Someone who was a relative unknown.

The most important factor was that Sarah Palin's résumé suggested that she shared McCain's ethical world view and sense of righteous duty. Back in Alaska, she had run against Republicans just as often as she had run against Democrats. McCain had also been a longtime political foe of Alaska senator Ted Stevens, and choosing someone who came to power outside the Alaska good-old-boys network would be another way to stick it to the old codger. Moreover, Palin was a patriot who had an uncomplicated love of country and whose son had enlisted in the army. She was a kindred spirit to McCain—a fellow rebel, another maverick. The two seemed made for each other.

BIRDS OF A FEATHER

Born to Chuck and Sally Heath in Sandpoint, Idaho, on February 11, 1964, Sarah Louise Heath moved with her family to Alaska when she was three years old. The Heaths settled in Wasilla in 1971. The small town near Anchorage is where Sarah Heath went to school, fell in love, and married her high school sweetheart, Todd Palin, on August 29, 1988. She worked in television broadcasting off and on before becoming a full-time mother after the birth of her second child, in October 1990. The Palin family eventually grew to include five children: Track (born April 1989), Bristol (born October 1990), Willow (born July 1994), Piper (born March 2001), and Trig (the youngest, who was born in April 2008 with Down syndrome).

Palin entered politics as a PTA mom, joined the Wasilla City Council, and went on to serve two terms as mayor. But it was not until 2003, when she took on the powerful state chairman of her own party, that the qualities that would make her so attractive to McCain came into focus.

In 2003 Palin risked everything when she went public with her charges against Randolph "Randy" Ruedrich, the Alaska GOP state party chair who, since meeting her as mayor of Wasilla, had been a key player in grooming Palin for higher office. "I wasn't there when she was conceived," Ruedrich told me jokingly. "I just got involved shortly thereafter."

An intelligent, quick-witted political operator, Ruedrich had been supportive of Palin in her unsuccessful bid for the lieutenant governor's post in 2002. And Ruedrich had made sure that Frank Murkowski considered Palin as his Senate replacement when he returned to Alaska to become governor that same year. When Murkowski decided to send his daughter Lisa to the Beltway instead, he still needed to figure out what to do with Palin. Ruedrich had an idea. Murkowski could appoint Palin to the Alaska Oil and Gas Conservation Commission (AOGCC). A seat on the obscure and highly technical board required no particular skill set. The AOGCC met in Anchorage, so the Palins would not have to move. Ruedrich thought it would be a good opportunity for Palin to learn about Alaska's main industry of oil and natural gas extraction. Murkowski agreed and appointed Palin to the commission on February 18, 2003. He appointed Ruedrich on the same day. Ruedrich had a background in the oil and gas industry and thought he could serve as Palin's tutor on energy issues. That wasn't how it turned out.

One of Palin's jobs on the commission was to supervise ethics. She began to receive complaints that Ruedrich, who hadn't given up his duties as state party chair, was conducting party business on the job. Palin passed the complaints on to Murkowski's office, but Murkowski had a tin ear and did not pay any mind. Palin grew frustrated. Like McCain, Palin becomes self-righteous when she confronts individuals who offend her idealistic sensibilities. She felt that Ruedrich was behaving inappropriately and none of the higher-ups were doing anything about it. The whole situation felt wrong. Either Murkowski would act or Palin would.

Palin went to the press. The *Anchorage Daily News* began publishing articles that repeated the charges against Ruedrich. Palin told the media that Ruedrich was conducting party business during commission hours and that he had forwarded a confidential commission document to a lobbyist associate. The punishing attacks on Ruedrich's reputation became unbearable. He resigned from the AOGCC on November 8, 2003. The grand experiment—Ruedrich mentoring the future state GOP star Sarah Palin—was a total failure. It had lasted less than eight months.

Ruedrich still maintains his innocence. Over caribou sausage, eggs, and coffee in 2009, he explained how Palin's accusations had been "completely without merit." He said the idea that he'd been conducting party business from his office was ludicrous.

The lawyers thought otherwise. Ruedrich handed me a photocopy of his settlement with the Alaska attorney general's office. As part of the deal, Ruedrich admitted that he had "used state facilities and state equipment on occasion to engage in partisan political activity while serving as a commissioner of the AOGCC." This referred to twenty-six e-mails that allegedly constituted "party business." Many of these, Ruedrich said, were e-mails that he received at his state account and forwarded to his personal account. Others were a mix of party business and official business that he forwarded from his personal account to his state account.

The claim that Ruedrich had sent confidential information to an energy lobbyist was an "absolute lie," he said. But, in the agreement with the state attorney general's office, Ruedrich admitted that he had done exactly what Palin accused him of doing. Ruedrich told me he had been appalled at a memo written by a "staff lawyer" that took Greenpeace's side in a fight over gas development in the Matanuska-Susitna (Mat-Su) Valley. He sent it to a friend. "It doesn't make it right," he acknowledged, "but it doesn't make it novel, either."

Ruedrich left the state government in 2003, but Palin was not finished with him. From her post on the AOGCC, she continued to pressure the Murkowski administration to mount a formal investigation into her former ally. The crusade damaged her relationship to the state GOP apparatus, in some cases beyond repair. But Palin's conception of politics always seems to have gone beyond party, which is one reason she appealed to John McCain.

Palin demanded that Murkowski's attorney general, Gregg Renkes, state whether an investigation into Ruedrich's alleged wrongdoing was under way. Renkes refused. On January 16, 2004, Palin resigned from the AOGCC to protest what she saw as the establishment's coddling of Ruedrich.

Governor Murkowski's handling of the affair caused him considerable political harm. Of course the state was looking into Ruedrich. The two parties agreed to a settlement on June 22, 2004. Ruedrich admitted to three charges: conducting partisan politics from an appointed office, sending a confidential commission memo to a third party, and breaking his promise not to conduct party business during the workday. He paid a substantial $12,000 fine as punishment, but he was able to retain his post as state GOP chairman.

Plenty of Alaska Republicans, including many in the Murkowski administration, saw Ruedrich as the victim of a political witch hunt. Ruedrich's supporters argued that state Democrats and their allies in the media had targeted Ruedrich in order to sideline him during the 2004 election campaign, when voters would have to decide whether to keep Lisa Murkowski in the U.S. Senate. Palin disagreed with this analysis. She called for Ruedrich to be sacked as GOP chair, but no one listened to her. She flirted with the idea of challenging Lisa Murkowski in the 2004 Senate primary, then decided against it. Instead she refused to endorse Murkowski and thus created yet another intraparty enemy.

Like McCain, Palin seemed to revel in holding members of her own party to account. In December 2004, when the *Anchorage Daily News* broke the story that Attorney General Renkes had negotiated a trade deal with Taiwan benefiting a coal company in which he held stock, citizen Palin went ballistic. She teamed up with Democratic state representative Eric Croft—the same Eric Croft who would later attack her relentlessly— and publicly called for the state personnel board to investigate.

Governor Murkowski paid no attention. He turned to outside counsel to look at Renkes's actions. The attorney general had disclosed his stockholdings in public filings but hadn't told Murkowski about the apparent conflict of interest. On January 25, 2005, the governor's handpicked outside lawyer, respected former U.S. attorney Robert Bundy, released his findings. Bundy's conclusion was that although Renkes's actions had been improper—he had violated the law by not asking for ethics counsel prior to dealing with Taiwan—the amount of money involved was not enough to constitute an illegal conflict of interest. The next day Murkowski said he would reprimand Renkes.

Yet Palin and Croft continued to hit the governor hard in media appearances, press quotations, and op-ed articles. One article in particular is worth noting. Writing in the *Anchorage Daily News* on the Renkes scandal, Palin noted that "[i]t's said the only difference between a hockey mom and a pit bull is lipstick." The line would go on to become her catch phrase, a felicitous way to describe her unique combination of normality and toughness. In mid-December 2004, Palin and

Croft lodged a formal complaint against Renkes with the state personnel board. That meant another investigation and the possibility of a harsh sanction. It was too much for the embattled attorney general. On February 5, 2005, Renkes resigned his office.

A NEW BEGINNING

The resemblances between McCain's and Palin's political styles are uncanny. When she encountered troubling moral situations, Palin gambled and chose the more perilous course of action: speaking out. For her, party and ideology were not the most important considerations. Her overwhelming imperative was to rectify perceived injustices—even if that meant tearing apart the state GOP.

Palin boldly took on the Murkowski Republican machine. Frank Murkowski had been a decent senator but he was a terrible governor. He was not a bad person. He did not seek out embarrassment. He simply had an anti–Midas touch. Everything he came into contact with turned to dirt. "Frank was a very clumsy governor," Paulette Simpson, the former president of the Alaska Federation of Republican Women, told me. "But not corrupt."

Murkowski reached the point of no return in October 2005, when Alaska's department of natural resources commissioner, Tom Irwin, wrote a memo criticizing the governor's relationship with the oil industry. The memo leaked to the press. Irwin attacked Murkowski's plan to build a natural gas pipeline. Murkowski was a longtime proponent of the gas line, which would stretch from Alaska's North Slope to the port of Valdez.

Murkowski was not the gas line's only supporter. For a quarter century Alaskans had been trying to build it, and the project was a top priority for the Murkowski administration. But the takeaway from

Irwin's memo was that the governor had been colluding with the energy companies to shut everyday Alaskans out of the debate. Irwin was a highly regarded figure. His criticism threatened to scuttle Murkowski's approach.

Murkowski responded to the memo with his typical subtlety, sensitivity, and tact. He fired Irwin. The decision was made entirely out of spite. Murkowski had no good reason to dump Irwin, especially in such a clumsy manner. The dismissal was a new low for the governor's administration. The state media swarmed over him.

When Murkowski terminated Irwin's employment, six members of the natural resources commissioner's staff resigned in protest. This bold rebuke heightened the controversy. Murkowski was already unpopular. Polls released during the summer had revealed him to be the second-most-disliked governor in America, with a disapproval rating at around 66 percent. Only Ohio's Bob Taft, under indictment for corruption, scored worse. Alaska was primed for a populist revolt. The feeling in the state was one of uneasiness. There was outrage at incumbent politicians and a widespread sense that the political class had been shortchanging voters in order to cozy up to the energy producers.

On October 18, 2005, Palin announced to her friends, family, and supporters that she would enter the primary for governor. "She decided to follow her heart," Anchorage-based pollster David Dittman told me. "She doesn't care. She does what she feels is the right thing. She believes she has a purpose." And in the fall of 2005 her purpose was clear: sink Frank Murkowski.

Murkowski's idleness maximized the chances that his career would end in 2006. He waited until the last minute to say he was running for a second term. His announcement did not arrive until May 2006, months after Palin had entered the arena.

The delay proved costly. Rather than line up support and cash and do what he could to salvage his junky reputation, Murkowski dithered. A third candidate, former state senator John Binkley, didn't have Palin's pull on Republican voters. Over Murkowski's term, Palin had gone from the governor's supporter to his most persistent critic. "She became the anti-Frank," political strategist Willis Lyford said in an interview.

Palin ran for governor on a nonideological and nonpartisan platform. She emphasized three issues: ethics, bipartisanship, and a new gas line agreement that would put Alaskans ahead of the energy industry. A Democrat could have campaigned along similar lines. Yet Republican primary voters understood that Palin's instincts favored small government, and her strong commitment to social conservatism was obvious. The trust Republicans put in Palin gave her room to maneuver. Her platform offended no one other than the oil companies and the Alaska GOP elites who had helped her career—and expected her to help them in return.

On primary day, August 22, 2006, Palin trounced the man who had wanted her to run for lieutenant governor four years earlier. She took 51 percent of the vote, John Binkley got 30 percent, and Murkowski won a dismal 19 percent. The drubbing of the incumbent governor was unambiguous. Palin had brought down a fixture of Alaskan politics. Not because she was some millionaire who had the resources to spend tons of money on quixotic political crusades. Not because the state GOP used her as its tool to dump Murkowski. Just the opposite. The only tools Palin had were her moral compass and plain-spoken charm. Like John McCain, she was the triumphant underdog.

A REFORMER WITH RESULTS

McCain would also have been drawn to the manner in which Palin governed. Governor Palin's achievements spoke to Americans' concerns over the high price of energy and entrenched corruption in government. She had promised to sign a law to replace Governor Murkowski's natural gas pipeline effort, which had been negotiated in secret between the governor's office and the Big Three oil companies. Murkowski's plan "went much further than was necessary" to entice the producers, Palin's energy adviser Joe Balash told me. "They tried to choke the producers with cash to get them to build the pipeline."

It was up to Palin to fix things. Several principles shaped her thinking on the gas line. Her goal was to have a deal with transparency, competition, and innovation. The process had to be accessible to the public. The companies would have to compete for the privilege of building the pipeline. And the winning plan would have to be able to accommodate future exploration and development. "We were concerned that Alaska wasn't getting all it wanted from the oil producers," former state senator Gene Therriault said in an interview.

The Murkowski plan was a giveaway to Big Oil that left the state with little wiggle room. Alaska would subsidize the pipeline's construction and not expect anything in return. Palin's bill opened up the bidding. The energy companies would have to apply to the state for the right to build the gas line. Each application would have to meet the state's tough standards. Murkowski's program had nixed taxing the gas revenues. Palin's left that option open but did not determine tax rates in advance. The state would have maximum flexibility to earn maximum rewards. Alaskans liked Palin's bill, which was called the Alaska Gasline Inducement Act (AGIA). The energy giants hated it. "We had an expectation that we'd have to water it down," Balash said.

The old guard still had influence in the state senate. "They were pushing it farther toward the oil companies' position than we wanted," Palin adviser John Bitney told me. A watered-down AGIA, or an AGIA that failed to pass altogether, would have been a considerable setback for Palin. The energy industry would have seen her as another pushover. But if she got her way, she would have wide latitude to govern Alaska the way she wanted. "There was no guarantee that it would totally go through," Bitney said.

Then, with two weeks to go in the legislative session, the FBI raided the homes of figures associated with the Veco energy services company. The indictments came down on May 4, 2007, when Palin was at a town hall meeting in Barrow, near the Arctic Circle—a BlackBerry-free zone. The local police arrived and asked to speak to her. She had a phone call, they said. It was the FBI. The bureau wanted to give the governor a heads-up about the raids. Palin took the call, responded politely and calmly, and returned to the business at hand.

That was when Palin's team knew AGIA was theirs.

The hint of illegality among influential figures in the energy industry was decisive. Up to that point, Palin had been a popular novice who was going to have to negotiate with more experienced hands in the legislature and the conglomerates. Not anymore. Alaskans were so disgusted by the incestuous relationship between the political class and the energy companies that they did not care whether the companies' interests were included in the pipeline bill. And the legislature was fearful of a public backlash, so it wasn't about to challenge the governor. Palin could get whatever she wanted. AGIA passed a week later.

The next item on Governor Palin's agenda was ethics reform. The situation Palin inherited from Murkowski was rife with justified suspicion regarding state lawmakers' intentions and relationships. Palin had become famous in Alaska for leading the outcry against perceived wrongdoing. She needed to live up to her reputation. For the public to take her seriously, she had to make some effort to revise the laws governing official conduct. "Alaskans no longer trusted their government," Joe Balash said. "And they needed to."

The major obstacle to passing the ethics bill was the number of people who wanted credit for it. After the 2006 election, and amid the ongoing FBI investigation into Veco, everyone who still held power wanted to jump in and own a piece of the good-government issue. Palin's first step was to ask two lawyers, Democrat (and future Palin foe) Ethan Berkowitz and Republican Wev Shea, to draft a memo outlining the changes to current law that needed to be made. The two men held reputations as fierce critics of the status quo in Juneau, but Palin's fellow Republicans were unhappy with her decision. Palin ignored the complaints and adopted the lawyers' recommendations. The new governor appeared to feed on criticism. "She's a very strong person," John Bitney told me. "Mentally and physically, she's tough." The final draft legislation, known as House Bill 109, passed on May 12, 2007. No one voted against it.

After ethics reform passed, Palin confronted the energy companies once more. ACES, or Alaska's Clear and Equitable Share, revised the state's oil tax for the first time in years. This was one area where Palin owed Murkowski, who had done most of the heavy lifting the previous year. He had spent much of 2006 persuading the legislature to switch from a tax on gross revenue to a tax on profits, and he had succeeded. There was plenty of criticism, however, some of it from Palin during the campaign. She said she had problems with the legislation but would wait to see how much revenue the tax generated for the state.

When the first numbers came in, in April 2007, Palin was disappointed. Murkowski's tax had underperformed substantially. At a time of record oil prices, the new tax law had failed to capture hundreds of millions of dollars in revenue. The previous law had also been passed during a time when scandal, guilty pleas to bribery, and rampant cronyism dominated the headlines. The oil companies had bested the Alaska political establishment for the umpteenth time. For Palin, Joe Balash said, "Some things are right and some things are wrong. She prefers to be in that black-and-white area. Gray makes her uncomfortable. And this was a black-and-white issue."

Palin instructed Balash to go back to the drawing board and rework the tax, but to keep it based on profits and not gross income. The new proposal also had to be transparent, and the state had to be guaranteed a certain revenue floor if oil prices tumbled. Palin might not have been a policy egghead, but she knew where to find the eggheads and was eager to consult with them. "We don't change our oil and gas tax too often," Gene Therriault told me. "It was a tough lift, and the governor and her team got it done."

The fight over ACES illustrated Palin's central governing challenge. She was an outsider, a critic of her own party whose political fortunes depended on a coalition of Democrats and a few "Palinista" Republicans. "The breakdown," Therriault said, "was between those who had blind allegiance to the oil industry and those who could separate one's pro-oil position from one's position as owner of the resource." Governor Palin's most vociferous critics were the establishment Republicans like State Senator Lyda Green, who felt that she had betrayed her own party and was behaving like an antidevelopment Democrat. Palin, these Republicans said, was in the game only for herself. What the critics did not understand was that Palin could not imagine herself as in the game for the Republican "team." She saw herself working on behalf of the people of Alaska.

Palin called a special session of the legislature to consider ACES. At the end of 2007, the bill was sitting in the House Finance Committee, going nowhere. The committee chairman, Republican Mike Chenault, wasn't moving on the bill.

One day, the story goes, the governor was speaking to some reporters in her office. One of them asked her, *Why is Chenault blocking*

ACES? Palin said, *Good question! I don't know. Let's go ask him!* She took the reporters down the hall to Chenault's office, where they confronted him. The episode damaged the governor's relationship with Chenault beyond recognition. But the personal relationship wasn't what mattered to Palin. What mattered was (a) Chenault's opposition to her legislation and (b) his refusal to explain his opposition publicly. Palin wanted Chenault to know she disapproved.

"She's not above breaking eggs," Joe Balash said, with a small smile. Governor Palin signed the new tax into law on December 19, 2007.

Sarah Palin is "very effective in putting together a team," Gene Therriault told me. "She doesn't have a problem with bringing in different people with expertise. She operates like a CEO: surround yourself with knowledgeable people and direct them." For the first two years of Palin's term, the CEO model worked smoothly. When gas prices skyrocketed in the summer of 2008, Palin became a well-known proponent of domestic energy exploration and production. Then she used the gusher of revenues from the new oil tax to send every Alaskan a $1,200 energy rebate. Her approval ratings were upwards of 80 and 90 percent. She was probably the most popular Republican politician in America.

This was a political portfolio tailor-made to appeal to John McCain.

THE VETTING

Initially there were twenty names on McCain's vice presidential list. For each potential candidate, attorney A. B. Culvahouse's vetting team put together a forty- to fifty-page analysis for the senator; his chief speechwriter and senior adviser, Mark Salter; campaign manager Rick Davis; and chief strategist Steve Schmidt.

By late June the list had been pared down to six contenders. Palin did not emerge as a serious possibility until late in the process. She was the last name added to the final six. According to Dan Balz and Haynes Johnson's book, *The Battle for America 2008,* the other finalists were Connecticut Senator Joe Lieberman, Pawlenty, Romney, New York City mayor Michael Bloomberg, and Florida governor Charlie Crist.

McCain wanted his friend Joe Lieberman on the ticket. The two men are strong security hawks, and what matters most to McCain is national defense. Moreover, Lieberman would make the ticket bipartisan. Choosing the Connecticut senator would demonstrate McCain's commitment to national unity in troubled times. And as Al Gore's vice presidential nominee in 2000, Lieberman had already run the media gauntlet. Joe Biden would not intimidate him. The veep debate would be feisty and combative. "John wanted Lieberman for a long time," a senior McCain adviser told me. "And everybody was pushing back on that for the obvious reason."

The reason was that Lieberman was a pro-choice Democrat. The only constellation of issues on which he aligned with the GOP was foreign policy. He opposed tax cuts. He vigorously supported government spending and pro-union initiatives. The deal breaker was his strong advocacy for abortion rights. The GOP had been a pro-life party for a generation, and the party relies on pro-life activists for volunteers and donations. Inviting Lieberman to join the ticket would have split the party. The convention would have been a disaster. Conservatives already mistrusted McCain. If he had nominated a Democrat to the ticket, they might have tried to block Lieberman's nomination from the convention floor. And that would have led to a Republican Party even more demoralized than it already was. So Lieberman was out.

Culvahouse sent the vice presidential finalists an in-depth questionnaire with more than seventy queries, and asked them for seven years of tax returns as well as copies of articles, books, and speeches. The written questionnaire asked about issues such as infidelity and prostitution, but if a candidate wanted to discuss something without committing it to print, he or she could let Culvahouse know, and he would be sure to take up the topic in the oral interview. Culvahouse's goal was for the prospects to be prepared for what was coming.

Palin was the last candidate who Culvahouse examined. The interview was over the phone and lasted close to three hours. The governor was "very forthcoming, disarming," a source present on the phone call told me. And she was no dummy. Palin knew that O'Melveny & Myers represented ExxonMobil in its litigation against Alaska. *I hope you're not going to serve me papers,* Palin joked to Culvahouse. The veteran lawyer, whose first job in Washington was with the Republican senator Howard Baker of Tennessee, admired the newcomer from up north. "The landscape of Alaska was littered with the carcasses of Republican bulls she had emasculated," a person involved in the vetting process said in an interview.

In the questionnaire, Palin had written that there was one thing she wanted to discuss solely over the phone. She wasted no time getting to the topic once the interview began. Palin explained that her daughter Bristol recently had told her that she was pregnant, that she was going to keep the baby, that she was due in December, and that she and her boyfriend were considering marriage. "She didn't pull any punches," the person involved in the vetting said.

To hear people close to the process describe it, the interview was comprehensive and detailed. The topics discussed included Palin's college record (had she been asked to leave any of the many schools she attended? No); her husband's twenty-year-old DUI arrest; the controversial Bridge to Nowhere earmark; the nature of any relationship with the Alaskan Independence Party (there wasn't any); and a brewing political scandal over the firing of the Alaska commissioner of public safety (so-called Troopergate). When Culvahouse asked about infidelity, Palin's response was clear: absolutely not, she said. Culvahouse thought that Palin came across as genuine and sincere. He asked her why she wanted to be vice president. He asked her whether she would authorize—should she at some point assume the role of president—a drone attack on Osama bin Laden's position if it meant that some civilians would also be killed. Palin told him that she would authorize the attack. But, she added, she would also ask forgiveness for taking innocent life. Her primary obligation, Palin said, would be to defend the country. Culvahouse thought her answer was spectacular. He asked her if she would be willing to use nuclear weapons to defend America. Her answer was yes.

The interview made a strong impression. "She clearly was still offended at what she saw on the Alaska Oil and Gas Conservation Commission," the source on the phone call told me. "She came across as a steward of the land and the environment, but also very determined to unlock Alaska's oil and gas resources. She used the term 'public servant' in a way that suggested she did not view the job as an entitlement. She just wasn't a business-as-usual-type person. She said, 'Look, there's a lot that I don't know. There's a lot I'd need help with.' But she had a humble confidence. She said that she was a fast learner, and that she surrounded herself with good people." After the interview, Culvahouse had a strong feeling that Palin was a front-runner for the job.

Then, on August 23, the Obama campaign announced via text message that Delaware senator Joe Biden had joined the Democratic ticket as the vice presidential nominee. Biden was a Washington fixture whose foreign policy experience as Senate Foreign Relations Committee chairman added a sort of heft to Obama's light résumé. The media widely praised Obama's decision, as per usual.

Meanwhile, as the Democrats held a successful convention in Denver, the McCain campaign's senior staff met in Arizona, where they weighed their own vice presidential options. On August 24, 2008, as she walked the grounds of the Alaska State Fair, Palin got a call from McCain, who invited her to Arizona. Palin arrived in Flagstaff on August 27, the day Biden addressed the Democratic convention. According to Robert Draper's "The Making (and Remaking) of McCain," published in the October 22, 2008, *New York Times Magazine,* Palin came face-to-face with Salter and Schmidt and talked to them about Bristol's pregnancy and the Alaska state legislature's Troopergate inquiry.

Around this time, Culvahouse told McCain about his Palin interview. Culvahouse said Palin would be a high-risk, high-reward choice. The risk was the possibility that Palin wouldn't be ready for the job on Inauguration Day 2009. Nor was Culvahouse sure how Palin's daughter's pregnancy would play politically. Privacy vanishes when you become a major party's vice presidential nominee. Keeping the news secret would be difficult. Probably impossible. Conservative Christians might respond in unexpected ways.

The reward was that Palin would upset the entire race. She would come across as a fresh face. She would be a powerful symbol for change, for not doing business as usual, for not tolerating people who violate the public trust. She was authentic, direct, young, pretty, and charming. She had demonstrated real courage and boldness in leadership and in her approach to politics. There was a growing list of Republicans, Democrats, and oil executives she'd defeated to prove it.

Palin also had an excellent grasp of what was, at that moment, the dominant issue in American politics. Palin's major legislative achievement was a gas pipeline. She'd make a great spokeswoman for more domestic carbon energy. Record gas prices had put Obama and the Democrats on the defensive. They wanted to limit the exploration and development of carbon-based fuels, preferring to subsidize alternatives, like wind, solar, and biomass energies. But many Americans wanted relief from high gas prices sooner rather than later, and felt that carbon extraction was the most realistic way to do it. In an August 2008 CNN poll, for instance, 69 percent of the respondents favored more offshore drilling.

On August 28, Palin met John McCain at his ranch in Sedona. The two had encountered each other only once before, at the National Governors Association meeting in D.C. in early 2008. To say they barely knew each other would be the polite way of putting it. They had no relationship whatsoever. According to Robert Draper's article, during this second meeting McCain took Palin on a tour of the ranch. Then Palin met McCain's wife, Cindy. McCain and his wife discussed the decision in private. When they were finished, he called in his top advisers. Knowledgeable sources told me that at that point two choices remained: Pawlenty and Palin. Salter, the speechwriter, preferred Pawlenty. McCain and his top strategist, Schmidt, preferred Palin. The vote was two to one. Palin was the pick.

Palin accepted. The campaign spirited her to Dayton, Ohio, where she'd make her debut the next morning. Meanwhile, the Palin family boarded a plane in Alaska to meet her in the Lower 48. Sarah Palin's new job was a closely guarded secret.

SURPRISE ATTACK

The McCain campaign sacrificed strategy in favor of tactics, and ignored potential long-term problems in order to concentrate on short-term gains. (The Obama strategy was the complete opposite.) Nowhere was this more true than in the vice presidential selection process, when Palin's possible downsides were all secondary to a tactical desire for secrecy and surprise.

One of the campaign's chief objectives was winning the daily news cycle—feeding the beast with a steady diet of rapid response and opposition research so that the day ended with McCain looking good and Obama looking ugly. Meanwhile, the campaign waged a small war against the media's undeniable pro-Obama bias. Part of that assault included hiring Michael Goldfarb, my friend and colleague at the *Weekly Standard.* Goldfarb's job initially was to write a blog poking fun at Obama's inconsistencies and the media's inanities. His duties and prominence grew over time.

Goldfarb joined the campaign in June 2008 as deputy communications director. He was a huge Palin fan and had long thought that she would make a great vice president. Indeed, his support for Palin was something of a joke inside the campaign. Folks at McCain headquarters did not take the governor very seriously. Goldfarb told me that, at communications meetings in the early summer of 2008, he would push for Palin to be used as a McCain surrogate, and people would laugh him out of the room.

By the beginning of August, however, Goldfarb had gotten the campaign brass to agree. Palin could now appear on television on McCain's behalf. Before that ever happened, though, the governor tripped up. Goldfarb was floored on August 4 when he saw that Palin had released a statement praising Senator Obama's energy plan. "It is gratifying to see Senator Obama get on board," Palin said in the release, referring to her cherished gas pipeline project. Here was another example of Palin's bipartisan credentials.

For his part, Goldfarb was shocked. The statement had ruined his efforts to get Palin stumping for McCain. His bosses indefinitely shelved the idea of Sarah Palin, campaign surrogate. Headquarters returned to normal business. No one had a clue that Palin was on the vice presidential shortlist.

Everyone was in the dark because the entire search process had been cloaked in secrecy. Obama's surprise choice of Joe Biden for vice president had impressed McCain's top advisers. They admired how the Obama campaign had kept a lid on the decision through tight lips and a little misdirection. They wanted a surprise of their own. Palin's unveiling would be a huge *gotcha* moment. McCain's supporters would be thrilled at the novel and exciting choice. The media would be completely unprepared. The pick would overturn the media narrative so far: the youthful, "postpartisan," African American Democrat against the old, crusty inheritor of the Bush legacy. With Palin, the media would have to cope with a young, brash, take-no-prisoners Republican. They would have no idea what to do. They would run around like headless chickens. It would be great.

All the stealth and surprise worked. The Democratic National Committee operated a Web site, The Next Cheney, attacking all the likely vice presidential prospects. Palin was nowhere to be found. As journalist and author Gregg Easterbrook noted in his February 10, 2009, ESPN.com column, "Ten days before John McCain made his vice presidential choice, Politico.com declared the pick was 'certain' to be either Mitt Romney or Tim Pawlenty. Seven days before, *Time* magazine said it had 'confirmed' with 'senior sources' that Romney would be chosen. The day before the choice, the *New York Times* said McCain would choose Romney, Pawlenty, or Joe Lieberman. No dark horse candidate, the *Times* said, was under consideration."

As late as Thursday, August 28, the McCain communications team had no idea whom McCain had picked. Rumors flew around headquarters about planes coming in from Alaska, but there were also planes flying elsewhere to keep the press confused. Goldfarb's boss Matt McDonald told him the news around 10 a.m. on August 29: PALIN!

"I doubt any other politician would have made a choice like that," a senior McCain adviser told me.

"Nobody's ever seen a surprise pick like that," Goldfarb said. "Nobody had any idea, and people were p.o.'d about it. The press was furious. They had no research. They had nothing to report. They looked like a bunch of fools."

Dan Balz and Haynes Johnson write that the Dayton, Ohio, rally where McCain announced Palin that Friday morning was the largest of his campaign. Fifteen thousand people showed up. They went crazy as Palin and her family walked out on stage. They barely knew who the woman was—how could they have known? She came from Alaska, for goodness' sake!—but that wasn't a concern. There was something about her, something ineffable, that drew people to her.

The debut was a complete success. Palin betrayed no sense of unease at the crowd or the role she had accepted. She had a natural instinct for oratory. She never rushed. She cracked a joke about how that day was her twentieth wedding anniversary, and how she had promised Todd a little surprise. (August 29 is also McCain's birthday.) When she told the crowd how her son Track couldn't make it to Dayton because his army brigade was preparing to deploy to Iraq, there were chants of "USA! USA! USA!" "I never really set out to be involved in public affairs, much less to run for this office," Palin said. "My mom and dad both worked at the local elementary school, and my husband and I, we both grew up working with our hands. I was just your average hockey mom in Alaska."

The speech included a concise description of the vice presidential nominee's political career: PTA mom, city councilwoman, mayor, ethics officer on the AOGCC, governor. Palin explained that, for her, the "common good" mattered more than party or any other particular interest. The speech contained no mention of abortion or gun rights. The focus was on energy and ethics, reducing spending, returning tax revenues to the people, and having a wise and tested commander in chief. "I know that when Senator McCain gave me this opportunity, he had a shortlist of highly qualified men and women," Palin said. "And to have made that list at all—it was a privilege. And to have been chosen brings a great challenge."

She had no idea just how great the challenge would be.

Mike Murphy ran John McCain's 2000 presidential campaign and remained an informal adviser to the senator until the summer of 2008. He immediately criticized the choice. He was worried about the campaign's motivations. "They hated the media so much," Murphy told me. "They were so happy they screwed the media on this. They forgot that the media would bite 'em like a dog."

CHAPTER TWO
The Feral Beast: The Media Go Wild

WHEN Sarah Palin strode onto the stage in Dayton, the media did not know how to react. They were completely unprepared. No one knew anything about her. The choice so disturbed the media that a subgenre of Palin literature quickly emerged dealing solely with how John McCain could possibly have arrived at such an (in their view) ridiculous decision. There was, for example, the *New Yorker*'s Jane Mayer, who spun thousands of words trying to get to the truth, which she thought had something to do with Palin and conservative media types pulling McCain's strings from behind the scenes. "That was like Jane Goodall going in and writing about [expletive deleted] apes mating in the jungle—they don't know what's going on," Goldfarb told the *Columbia Journalism Review* in January 2009. "They're writing from another planet."

The most common conspiracy theory was that the Palin candidacy had been cooked up by the editors at the magazine where I work. The only evidence in support of this hypothesis was that Palin had met with my bosses William Kristol and Fred Barnes when the annual *Weekly Standard* cruise stopped in Juneau in the summer of 2007. The hastily arranged meeting had been brief, but both Kristol and Barnes came away impressed. Barnes subsequently wrote an article for the *Standard* on Palin, published in July 2007. It remained one of the few profiles of the governor published in a national publication before she joined the GOP ticket more than a year later. No wonder that political writers, who have an exaggerated view of their own status and power, felt as though the *Standard* had secured Palin's nomination. Since Barnes was one of the few journalists in America who knew who Sarah Palin was, surely he had something to do with her place on the ticket.

He didn't. McCain and his inner circle made the choice.

This did not stop the media from pretending otherwise. On October 10, 2008, the law-professor-turned-pundit Scott Horton wrote an article for the newly launched Daily Beast Web site arguing that William Kristol was the key figure behind the Palin pick. In the original version of the piece, Horton wrote that the Palin nomination had been concocted on "a cruise liner sponsored by the political journal the *Weekly Standard*" on which "editors and guests of the publication were treated to a reception" with Governor Palin. Horton wrote that a reporter for the British *Daily Telegraph* had interviewed "one of the participants in the Juneau junket, who said, 'She's bright and she's a blank page. She's going places and it's worth going there with her.'" Horton went on to say that "Palin's name appeared in fifty-seven *Weekly Standard* articles since the Juneau meeting."

This was all false. The Palin "reception" was not open to "editors and guests of the publication." It was a small, last-minute, slap-dash meeting that consisted of Kristol, Barnes, their wives, and a few others. Nor did the *Daily Telegraph* interview "one of the participants." The quote came from an anonymous source at the American Enterprise Institute in Washington, D.C. Furthermore, most of the "fifty-seven articles" in the magazine in which Palin's name was mentioned were published *after* Palin joined the McCain ticket. The *Daily Beast* later amended the piece. But not before embarrassing itself.

Palin might not have been known to the press, which rarely pays attention to political figures between the coasts, but she did have a reputation among some Republican and conservative elites. Chief McCain strategist Steve Schmidt, for example, had business connections to consultants in Anchorage who had only good things to say about Alaska's governor. If you were looking to disrupt the election narrative, as Team McCain was, and were also interested in reaching out to a group the GOP normally doesn't pay much attention to (women), then picking Palin wasn't an absurd course of action at all. Quite the opposite. The ranks of conservative women are relatively thin, and the ranks of pro-life conservative women with executive experience are even thinner. Yes, the choice was unexpected. It came out of left (right?) field. But it was not totally earth-shattering.

Unless you were part of the media. Because when the feral beast learned that Sarah Palin had joined the GOP ticket, it was confused. *Who was she? Where had she come from? What did she believe?* And most important: *Why weren't we prepared?* Shock set in, then embarrassment. Condescension came later. "If the media reaction is anything," *Newsweek* writer Eleanor Clift said on *The McLaughlin Group,* "it's been literally laughter in many places across newsrooms."

The forty-four-year-old pro-life mother of five, governor of America's largest state, the woman who brought down the Alaska GOP establishment—she had to be reduced, dissected, and molded into something fit for media consumption. In order for that to happen, however, the media needed to play catch-up. They didn't know the first thing about Palin other than that she was pro-life and had recently given birth to a Down syndrome child.

Immediately reporters started hitting the phones, typing furiously on their BlackBerrys, contacting everyone in Alaska with a telephone listing or an e-mail address. The press loves quoting academics, so interview requests inundated the University of Alaska Anchorage. A professor in the political science department, James Muller, told me he felt besieged. Nor was he alone. Every day was the same. Calls, calls, calls, e-mails, e-mails, e-mails. Interviews would continually be interrupted by reporters asking for more interviews. The beast was awake.

And it was hungry.

The self-appointed "elite" who populate America's newspapers, radio stations, and news networks are widely ignorant of their country. For the Alaskans fielding the reporters' calls, the media's shallowness was shocking. These folks all went to good schools, many of them graduated at or near the top of their class, but they could tell you more about the Prague neighborhood where they had lived during their year abroad than about the forty-ninth state of the country where they had been born and raised. Alaskans have told me about reporters who did not know that Juneau was Alaska's state capital, who were not sure whether Palin was governor, who had to be told the difference between oil and natural gas. One reporter wanted to know whether he needed a visa to travel to Alaska. The hacks meted out each question with a censorious and holier-than-thou attitude. Did they have snakes at Palin's church? Did she fake her pregnancy? What about evolution?

"They were looking for dirt," a professor at the University of Alaska Anchorage said.

Everybody was starting from scratch. The information vacuum became a space where the slimiest, nastiest, most baseless rumors flew around unencumbered by fact. Anyone who had the slightest connection to Alaska or Palin was—*presto!*—a reputable source. They didn't even have to give their real name. On September 5, 2008, writer Charley James published an article on LAProgressive.com that quoted "Lucille," who said she had heard Palin describe the 2008 Democratic primary results in this way: "So Sambo beat the b*tch." Lucille claimed to have been Palin's lunchtime waitress at a local restaurant when the governor made the improbable utterance. Yet there is absolutely no evidence confirming this story. The tale was hearsay without corroboration. This did not stop several liberal blogs from linking to it.

Palin's many critics dominated the coverage. Over the years the governor had stepped on a lot of toes, the owners of which now wanted to exact revenge. "As Mayor of Wasilla, Palin Cut Own Duties, Left Trail of Bad Blood" read the headline in the September 14, 2008, *Washington Post*. "Once Elected, Palin Hired Friends and Lashed Foes" read the headline on a September 14, 2008, *New York Times* piece. Guess which side supplied most of the quotes in that story? It wasn't her friends. (The *Times* piece, the newspaper's own public editor, Clark Hoyt, wrote on September 22, "never made the connection between style and results necessary to judge a politician who was overwhelmingly re-elected mayor and has an eighty percent approval rating as governor.")

"The *Times* and the *Post* went to Alaska and couldn't find a single person to say a kind thing about a governor with a sixty-five-percent-plus approval rating," a senior Palin campaign adviser told me. "Unbelievable."

One Wasillan, Anne Kilkenny, penned a ten-page e-mail that ended up being widely circulated over the Internet. It eventually became the template for most media outlets' Palin reportage. In reality, the Kilkenny e-mail is far less damning than it was made out to be. She wrote that Palin is "enormously popular," "smart," "energetic and hardworking," and "savvy." And she concluded: "[T]here's a lot of people who have underestimated her and are regretting it." Needless to say, these are not the words that factored into the media's reporting.

Kilkenny, a Democrat, is a town gadfly who claims to have attended every Wasilla City Council meeting during Palin's first year as mayor. Since her politics differ from Palin's, it is hardly a surprise that she would be critical. She disagreed with Mayor Palin's decisions on tax and spending issues, and especially over Palin's attempted firing of the town librarian. To liberals and the press, Kilkenny was a hero who had stood up against the troglodyte Palin. During an interview taped for the September 5 episode of NPR's *All Things Considered,* the NPR correspondent noted that Kilkenny took calls from "NBC, the *St. Petersburg Times,* and *People* magazine" while he and she conversed. John Nichols of the *Nation* reprinted Kilkenny's e-mail in its entirety on the lefty publication's Web site, describing Kilkenny as a "good citizen" who "clashed with Palin" when the mayor was "campaigning to ban books."

This was a gross overstatement of the actual controversy. The published accounts report that within a month of her election in 1996, Palin asked town librarian Mary Ellen Emmons how she felt about censoring public library books. Palin wanted to know whether a book could be kept behind the library counter where children couldn't find it on their own. Emmons said she opposed censorship, and Palin backed off. A careful politician, she was testing the limits of what the public found acceptable. She had plenty of supporters who felt that the public library shouldn't carry titles on adult matters like sex, especially in the open, but she wasn't about to pick a major fight over the issue. Kilkenny told the *New York Times* that Palin also raised removing controversial books from the library at a city council meeting, but no one else confirmed that story for the *Times.*

A widely circulated hoax e-mail purported to contain a list of the "books Palin tried to have banned," which included *A Wrinkle in Time* and the Harry Potter series. The list contained dozens of books, including several that were not even published when Palin was mayor. The hoax established Palin's reputation as a censor, someone not far from burning books outright. But anyone who calls Palin a censor is wrong. The episode with Emmons illustrates just the opposite, in fact. No one can name a single book that Palin ordered removed from the public library. It's true that Mayor Palin was willing to speak in solidarity with her social conservative supporters and bring up their concerns in conversations with public officials like Emmons. But a huge public debate over censorship wasn't worth the trouble.

The library stuff was a minor controversy at the time. The media hugely inflated it later to build a ridiculous case that Palin is a raving nut. Far more important to the people who lived in Wasilla was Palin's attempt to reshape the municipal government. Upon entering office, Palin demanded the resignations of the city officials associated with her predecessor, John Stein. The police chief, the librarian, and the directors of public works and finance all had to go. The changes touched off a huge argument. "She basically cleaned house," Stein told me.

Firing the librarian was too much even for Palin, who rehired Emmons a day after dismissing her. (Emmons left the job years later on her own volition and has repeatedly declined comment on Palin.) A second round of staff cuts came thereafter, when Palin fired the museum curator. Three ladies who worked at the museum—a small building next door to the equally small library—resigned in protest. The disruptions to the normal course of government upset so many people that a small group looked into whether Palin could be recalled from office. But the movement fizzled due to lack of interest.

Palin was within her rights as mayor to make the changes in personnel. She was running up against a persistent complaint about bureaucrats: once someone becomes ensconced in a government job, he often feels entitled to it for good. Any attempt to replace him becomes "political." Obviously it's political. We have elections to determine the composition of the government. And any change in government is messy. For the party that's being thrown out, the process usually resembles nothing more than the new political boss punishing his enemies and rewarding his friends. But as long as the executive follows the law, the opposition will have to live with temporary unemployment. Mayor Palin followed the law.

The personnel overhaul no doubt could have been handled differently and more ably. In retrospect, however, it was exactly the sort of public relations snafu one would expect from a first-time mayor. Yet the media ignored the broader issues entirely and instead focused on the question of whether Palin supported censorship. They adopted the extreme libertarian position—that no amount of censorship is ever justified—and inflated what had been a passing kerfuffle into a world-historical battle. There was no sense of balance. No sense of proportion.

COMMUNICATIONS BREAKDOWN

Rather than relate Palin's biography and accomplishments, the media reported extensively on whether the McCain campaign had properly vetted her. The question became an obsession for them. Reporters noted that the McCain campaign had not sent staff members to Alaska to pore over Palin's record. Correct. That's because senior campaign officials wanted to be sure that the vice presidential selection process remained a secret. The lawyers who vetted Palin are adamant that they examined her record closely and knew which aspects of her life would be controversial. "There's been nothing that's been mentioned about her that we weren't all over," one told me.

The problem was that the vetting file on Palin was never passed on to the McCain campaign's communications team. The decision was kept so secret that the folks tasked with responding to media inquiries about the vice presidential nominee were as uninformed as the press—sometimes more. At first, when responding to questions about Palin, even the McCain campaign relied on Fred Barnes's original July 2007 *Weekly Standard* article. The vetting process may have been thorough, but the equally important process of rolling out the vice presidential selection—knowing which parts of the nominee's biography to emphasize, having a list of accomplishments and trivia at the ready, being aware of possible lines of Democratic and media attack—was an absolute disaster.

The morning of August 29, about two hours before the Palin nomination was announced, one McCain staffer—I'll call him "Jack"—received a phone call from a campaign higher-up. The bigwig told Jack to put together a document listing the vice presidential candidate's accomplishments. Jack asked: *Who is it?* And the bigwig responded: *The most rumored person.*

Jack didn't know what to do, and asked: *Do you mean Governor Palin?* The reply: *Trust your instincts.* It was as if the campaign staffer was supposed to use the Force to determine his candidate's vice presidential nominee. Shortly thereafter, the staffer received another call with additional instructions: *Prepare your Romney material.* Utter confusion set in. The office was filled with rumors, including one about the Alaska governor. Before he took the second call, Jack had been working under the correct assumption that the pick was Palin. "The senior staff was playing disinformation games with the communications team,"

Jack told me. "No one was prepared to deal with any of the charges" against Palin.

Adding to the knowledge deficit was the fact that no one on the McCain communications staff had worked for Governor Palin. They had been with McCain since the beginning or had come from other, losing Republican presidential campaigns. If McCain had gone with Romney, for example, there would have been plenty of former Romney staffers on hand who could rebut the press's misconceptions about the former Massachusetts governor. The same goes for Fred Thompson or Rudy Giuliani (neither of whom was in serious contention). Palin's final rival for the nod, Governor Pawlenty, first met McCain in the 1980s and had spent day after day stumping on the senator's behalf. His staff and McCain's knew one another well. Responding to attacks and deflating myths about the Minnesota Wild–loving pol would have come much more easily. Not so with Palin. The communications team had trouble coming up with something as simple as an accurate list of her foreign travel. "We were vetting her through the campaign," the McCain staffer said.

Five things magnified the communications team's difficulty: (1) Alaska was far away from McCain headquarters in Crystal City, Virginia, which meant it was difficult to reach Palin's staff in Juneau and Anchorage (the four-hour time difference contributes to a communications lag); (2) Palin had many adversaries, most of whom were Republicans, so it was hard to get disinterested information on her; (3) the campaign team had hardly any access to a paper trail in Alaska, which meant the historical record was thin; (4) the media tend to chase fantastic stories down myopic, meaningless rabbit holes; and (5) as a general rule in presidential campaigns, chaos reigns. These disparate elements combined to send the McCain staff into a panic. They spent the week after Palin's selection in full defensive mode, fending off the feral beast. "The onslaught," Jack told me, "was more than anyone expected."

For instance, the notion quickly took hold over the press corps that Palin was a supporter of paleoconservative writer and commentator Patrick Buchanan, who unsuccessfully ran for the Republican presidential nomination in 1992 and 1996 (and then for president as the Reform Party nominee in 2000). Buchanan's positions on World War II, Israel, the Iraq war, social mores, and trade are outside the Republican mainstream. Support for Buchanan would have been a major political liability for Palin. This probably explains the almost giddy tone to the *Nation*'s Christopher Hayes's August 29 blog entry: "Remember when Pat Buchanan ran a number of hard-right, fringe campaigns for president in the late 1980s, 1990s and 2000? Well, guess who was supporting him." The inference Hayes wanted his readers to draw was Sarah Palin.

For evidence, Hayes quoted a 1999 Associated Press story describing a Buchanan visit to Alaska, where the author of *Right from the Beginning* and *The Great Betrayal* delivered a speech and signed some books. Palin was in the audience, wearing a Buchanan button. But after the story came out, Palin quickly wrote to the local paper saying that she had worn the button out of politeness and did not support Buchanan. It would have been odd for Palin to support Buchanan in 1999 anyway, as she was a registered Republican who backed Steve Forbes in the 2000 GOP primary, and Buchanan was severing his ties to the GOP. Hayes later issued multiple corrections to the item, which relied solely on presumption and also inaccurately stated that Buchanan had run for president "in the late 1980s."

None of this stopped the fiction from spreading. The original version of a Jonathan Alter column in *Newsweek* contained the false story, and Buchanan claimed on *Hardball with Chris Matthews* that Palin and her husband had supported him in 1996, though there is no evidence for this assertion, either.

On August 30, Florida Democratic congressman Robert Wexler issued a statement that read: "John McCain's decision to select a vice presidential running mate that endorsed Pat Buchanan for president in 2000 is a direct affront to all Jewish Americans. Pat Buchanan is a Nazi sympathizer with a uniquely atrocious record on Israel, even going as far as to denounce bringing former Nazi soldiers to justice and praising Adolf Hitler for his 'great courage.'" Wexler went on to accuse McCain of having "failed his first test of leadership" because he chose "a running mate who has aligned herself with a leading anti-Israel voice in American politics. It is frightening that John McCain would select someone one heartbeat away from the presidency who supported a man who embodies vitriolic anti-Israel sentiments." Completely false, yet Wexler never retracted his baseless and reprehensible smear.

That same day, Mark Bubriski, an Obama spokesman, wrote an e-mail to *Miami Herald* reporter Marc Caputo, who posted it on his blog. "Palin," Bubriski wrote, "was a supporter of Pat Buchanan, a right-winger or as many Jews call him: a Nazi sympathizer."

It was Michael Goldfarb's job to figure out whether there was any truth to the story. He was able to get Palin herself on the phone. *What's the deal?* he asked. *Did you or didn't you support Buchanan?* Palin's reply was blunt: *No. Absolutely not. I was part of Steve Forbes's campaign in 2000.* Goldfarb learned that while Palin did attend the Buchanan book signing and did wear the button in a gesture of goodwill, there was no documentation recording her political support for Buchanan in 1996 or 2000. Goldfarb had an uncomfortable realization as he set about debunking the Buchanan myth. Palin was caught in an information trap. "She has enemies everywhere in Alaska," Goldfarb told me. "And they are *all* Republicans. The upside had been that she'd worked with

Democrats. As soon as she's picked, though, there's no Democrat who'll say anything nice about her."

Another erroneous story about Palin was that she had been a member of the Alaskan Independence Party. The AIP is one of the largest third parties in the United States, and its platform calls for a vote on state independence. A party that calls for its state to leave the union may strike some readers as odd, but the AIP has an outsized role in Alaska politics. The party's success is a classic illustration of Alaskan opposition to, yet dependence on, the United States government. For successful political figures in the forty-ninth state, the AIP is a semi-fringe constituency that cannot be ignored. And when the far-left Daily Kos Web site began accusing Palin of membership in the party, political reporters in the Lower 48 took notice.

"That's what the American media reads," Goldfarb told me. "Daily Kos. That's their source."

The ABC News political reporter Jake Tapper called Goldfarb asking whether he could confirm that Palin had been a member of the AIP. The party's leadership was claiming as much. Once again, Goldfarb got on the phone to get an answer. Palin told the campaign that she hadn't been a member. She had delivered an innocuous video message to the AIP's 2008 convention. And in a separate video, the party's vice chairman, Dexter Clark, suggested that Palin had been a member. The facts were in dispute, as they often were during the period when Palin was first introduced to the American public. So, in order to answer Tapper's question, Goldfarb had a campaign staffer in Alaska dig up Palin's voter registration. The document proved that she had been a registered Republican since age eighteen.

The next day, however—September 2, 2008—the *New York Times'* Elisabeth Bumiller published a front-page story under the headline, "Palin Disclosures Raise Questions on Vetting." In the piece, Bumiller simply asserted that Palin had been a member of the AIP. The governor, she wrote, "was a member for two years in the 1990s of the Alaska[n] Independence Party." Around this time, in a CBS News report on the vetting process, one television correspondent said that "questions are flying about how much the McCain campaign knew about other issues like . . . reports that she participated in Alaska's Independence Party, which has called in the past for the state to secede from the union."

None of this was true. It did turn out that Todd Palin had briefly been a member of the AIP; that may have been the basis for Bumiller's mistaken claim that Sarah Palin was a member "for two years." Who knows? "The governor did appear at the AIP convention in 2000," Goldfarb wrote on his McCain Report blog, "*when the convention was held in Wasilla.* This would seem to be the only decent thing to do, given her responsibilities as *Mayor of Wasilla*" (emphasis in the original). A balanced, informed take on Palin would have been to say that her husband had been a member of the AIP and that she had been generous, perhaps even solicitous, toward the organization during her tenure as mayor and governor. But the media couldn't even approach a balanced take on the woman who had been air-dropped into their midst. They fell back on instinct. They seized the most salacious angle they could find.

When the press wasn't defacing the facts of Palin's biography, they were doing their best to minimize her accomplishments in office. For starters, the media echoed the Democrats' contention that Palin was somehow lying when she said she had "put" Governor Murkowski's plane "on eBay." The statement is literally true: Palin *did* put the jet up for sale on the electronic marketplace. No one bought the plane there, however. And because Palin never mentioned this relatively insignificant aspect of her story—the plane was later sold to a Valdez businessman in August 2007—the left pilloried her as a phony.

It's true that John McCain once said Palin had "sold" the jet on eBay "for a profit." This was a falsehood, probably the result of a staff miscommunication, that McCain did not repeat. For her part, however, Palin seems to have been extremely careful with the facts. The plane was "put" on eBay, not "sold" there. Even so, the whole flap is nitpicking to a ridiculous degree. Does it make one iota of difference whether the plane sold on eBay? The entire debate misses the point: Palin felt the jet was excessive and got rid of it. That should have been the end of the story, but the media barreled on, parsing every last syllable of Palin's statements, subjecting all her utterances to a degree of scrutiny that they reserved for her alone.

The badly managed McCain campaign's scramble for information left it vulnerable. "It was literally [working] from scratch," a McCain staffer told me. "We were doing the exact same thing the DNC was doing. While they were scrambling to attack, we were scrambling to defend."

The Democrats' onslaught against Palin centered on debunking her reformist credentials. Critics said Palin was a hypocrite because, as mayor of Wasilla, she had hired an Anchorage-based lobbyist to secure federal earmarks—direct, project-specific appropriations—for her town. The connection won Wasilla some $27 million during Mayor Palin's final years in office. Palin liked earmarks just fine when she was mayor and (later) governor, the critics said. Now that she's running for vice president, though, she pretends to hate the money.

The critics' charge of hypocrisy was absolute nonsense. Had they never observed a presidential campaign? It is a longstanding tradition that the vice presidential selection adopts the presidential nominee's positions. The vice presidential selection is at the bottom of the ticket, not the top, and that has to count for something. Palin's views on earmarks prior to her selection as McCain's veep were simply irrelevant. McCain is a vocal critic of earmark spending, so vice presidential candidate Palin would have to be one, too. Besides, a politician can always change her mind. Many have done so on more pressing matters than earmarks. And if Palin is guilty of hypocrisy on earmarks, then so was Barack Obama, who had requested no less than $740 million worth of earmarks during his tenure in the Senate. Obama had criticized wasteful spending while voting for some of the most pork-ridden bills in American history.

Palin's claim that as governor she had said "Thanks, but no thanks" to the Bridge to Nowhere drove liberals up a wall. The infamous earmark, first inserted into an omnibus spending bill in 2005, devoted funds to build a bridge from the Gravina Island airport to Ketchikan on Alaska's southeastern peninsula. For years, a ferry has shuttled travelers between the island and the mainland. But the Alaskan congressional delegation, which has never met an earmark it did not like, insisted that a bridge was necessary. The estimated cost was more than $300 million for a bridge to an island with a population of less than a hundred people.

The endeavor quickly became politically controversial. It was excellent fodder for jokes on late-night television about spendthrift Republicans. Despite the bad publicity, however, Alaska's congressman, senators, and Governor Murkowski engaged in a long battle with the rest of Congress to obtain funding for the bridge. The projected cost steadily expanded to around $400 million. John MacKinnon, Alaska's former deputy commissioner of transportation, told me that he realized during Governor Murkowski's administration that "there were better things to spend money on."

When she ran for governor in 2006, Palin expressed her support for the bridge. But she changed her position once in office. The budget she sent the state legislature in 2007 cut the state money appropriated for construction. Gradually it became clear to Palin that the entire project was doomed. In September 2007, she directed the Alaska Department of Transportation (ADOT) to find a less expensive alternative to the Gravina Island bridge. "She looked at it and determined the project was one we couldn't afford," MacKinnon said. The Bridge to Nowhere was no more.

The September 2007 policy reversal is the basis for Palin's claim that she told Congress "Thanks, but no thanks." Like her take on Murkowski's jet, Palin's statement is literally true. MacKinnon told me that the "Thanks, but no thanks" formulation is the accurate way to describe how Palin handled the problem. "Knowing how the governor speaks," he said, "she speaks like a regular person. And that's one of her appeals. She's saying, 'Thanks for some of the money to build the bridge, but we have higher priorities.'"

This was far more nuance than Democrats and the media could handle. Palin, they crowed, was taking credit for ending a project that she had originally supported—and still wanted federal dollars for her state in any case! Apparently the media are unaware that politicians occasionally change their positions, especially during the transition from candidate to officeholder. For his part, Barack Obama has reversed himself on—to name only a few examples—public financing for campaigns, taxing health care benefits, and immunity for telecommunications companies that participated in the terrorist surveillance program. The media treat Obama's reversals as signs of his sophistication and pragmatism, his smooth ability to adapt to changing circumstances. Palin's policy shifts, on the other hand, are characterized as lies and blatant acts of cynicism.

"I can spin it anyway you want it," Palin's former adviser John Bitney told me when I asked him about Palin's record on the Bridge to Nowhere. And Bitney is partly right: as always, the facts are more complicated and interesting than the prepackaged campaign narrative. The overriding truth, however, is that Palin was the chief executive who put the kibosh on the Bridge to Nowhere. Consider her low popularity ratings in Ketchikan, attributable to her killing the bridge. Consider how, on September 8, 2008, conservative blogger Charles Johnson discovered an Alaska Democratic Party Web site that read: "Gov. Sarah Palin said the $398 million bridge was $329 million short of full funding, and only $36 million in federal funds were set aside for it. She said it was clear Congress had little interest in spending any more money for it and that the state had higher priorities." The Web site, Johnson wrote, "mysteriously vanished" after Palin's debut, then reappeared under a different address. The Web site also said that the "State of Alaska officially abandoned the controversial project" in September 2007. Exactly. The governor of the state when the bridge was abandoned? You know who.

"[I]t is true that Palin declared an end to the project," the *Washington Post*'s Michael Dobbs wrote in a September 9, 2008, post on his Fact Checker blog. But, Dobbs went on, "that's beside the point." Really? Hard to believe, considering that all Palin ever said was that she did away with the bridge. But no, Dobbs continued. It "would be more accurate to say that she finally bowed to fiscal reality and congressional politics after a year as governor, and killed off a project that had become a national joke." Where Dobbs got the "after a year as governor" phrase is a mystery, since Palin told ADOT to forgo the bridge in September 2007, less than a year into her term. So Dobbs's statement was actually *less* accurate than Palin's. Moreover, Dobbs ascribed motivations to Palin that were a matter of supposition, not fact, and totally irrelevant to the empirical question of who cut off funding.

The reason the Bridge to Nowhere no longer sucks up taxpayer money is that Sarah Palin decided to end it. That is undeniable. Rather than report this, however, the press decided to highlight Palin's past support for the bridge in order to portray her as a conniving opportunist. Most galling of all, plenty of the reporters who wrote about Sarah Palin and the Bridge to Nowhere did so without mentioning that Barack Obama and Joe Biden both voted *for* the bill containing the original earmark. To the American media, then, Palin should get absolutely no credit for killing the bridge while Obama should receive no blame for helping to create it.

My Opponent's Youth and Inexperience

The Palin nomination sent both campaigns scrambling. As the McCain campaign hurried to gather enough background information to respond to egregious attacks, staff members also had to deal with internal tension. "Whether it was the Bridge to Nowhere, the AIP, the Buchanan stuff," a McCain staffer told me, "even if [vetting chief A. B.] Culvahouse had material, it was not passed down. Even if there was material, the four senior staffers were going five hundred miles an hour and didn't have time" to share it.

Shortly after McCain announced that Palin was joining the ticket, the Obama campaign responded. The initial release was harsh, impolitic, and ungracious. "Today," Obama spokesman Bill Burton said in a statement, "John McCain put the former mayor of a town of nine thousand with zero foreign policy experience a heartbeat away from the presidency." Obama understood that this was a misstep. He and Biden later issued another, kinder message to reporters. "We send our congratulations to Governor Sarah Palin and her family on her designation as the Republican nominee for vice president," it read. "It is yet another encouraging sign that old barriers are falling in our politics. While we obviously have differences over how best to lead this country forward, Governor Palin is an admirable person and will add a compelling new voice to this campaign."

The Obama campaign's second statement was well written and cordial. It was also smart politics, because Americans' first impression of Palin was positive. They liked this feisty newcomer. They wanted to know more about her. To cut against that opinion, as Burton's statement did, invited public rebuke. Better for Obama to wait and see how she performed.

And yet Burton's statement was revealing. The spokesman hit on two themes that would dominate liberal criticism of Palin: the governor's qualifications ("zero foreign policy experience") and her provenance ("the former mayor of a town of nine thousand"). The strategy of Palin's enemies was to portray her as a provincial hick who was out of her depth. Burton's words laid the foundation for such an assault.

Charges of inexperience had bedeviled Palin throughout her political career. She was said to be bush league when she ran for mayor, when she ran for lieutenant governor, when she ran for governor. "There was a lot of talk about the fact that I didn't have years of experience," Palin told *Sarah* author Kaylene Johnson. "But leadership shouldn't be based on years of public experience—it should be based on vision and example." Now the same talk was happening as she began her vice presidential campaign.

Burton's argument was that someone with "zero foreign policy experience" should not be "a heartbeat away" from the presidency. His sentiment has a long history. According to William Safire, in his 2008 *Safire's New Political Dictionary,* the expression "a heartbeat away" was used in a 1952 Adlai Stevenson attack on Eisenhower's vice presidential nominee, Richard Nixon. As payback, Safire writes, "Nixon supporters in the 1960 campaign took a leaf from Stevenson's text. They compiled a list of every one of vice presidential candidate Lyndon Johnson's votes against civil rights legislation as a representative and senator and circulated a flyer in black neighborhoods entitled 'Only a Heartbeat from the Presidency.'"

The late-nineteenth-century GOP boss Mark Hanna used a similar formulation to criticize Theodore Roosevelt's appointment as McKinley's vice president in 1900. Democrats used the "heartbeat" line against Dan Quayle in the 1988 presidential election. The formulation lives on, despite its lack of success in persuading voters.

The media glommed on to the experience critique and did not let go. "And now John McCain reaches out to somebody so young with so little experience," the ABC News anchor Charlie Gibson said on August 29. "We have a seventy-two-year-old nominee of the Republican Party . . . ," Matt Lauer of the *Today* show said the same day. "Although vice presidential candidates don't win or lose elections generally, this is a position a heartbeat away, and how are people going to feel about Sarah Palin in that situation?" CNN anchor John Roberts said, "She's only been in office for a couple of years now, which really raises the experience issue." CNN's Campbell Brown said, "Sarah Palin's only been governor for less than two years. Of all the Republicans out there, is she really the most qualified person to be commander in chief in a crisis?" On August 29, MSNBC ranter Keith Olbermann called Palin "the least experienced vice presidential candidate probably in American history."

Never mind the words of Bill Clinton, who said in August 2008 that "you can argue that nobody is ready to be president . . . You can argue that even if you've been vice president for eight years, that no one can be fully ready for the pressures of the office." For Palin's critics, her years on the Wasilla City Council, two terms as mayor, involvement in state politics, and twenty months as governor were insufficient prerequisites for a job whose only constitutional requirements are that you be at least thirty-five years old and a natural-born citizen of the United States, and whose only constitutionally specified duties are to serve as president of the Senate, cast tie-breaking votes there, and take over if the president is incapacitated or dies. Obviously it was worthwhile to examine Palin's résumé, and if one found it lacking, to oppose her vice presidential candidacy on that basis. But one should also note that Palin had about the same amount of experience as Calvin Coolidge and Theodore Roosevelt did when they were nominated to the vice presidency.

One should note, too, that the 2008 Democratic nominee for *president* had less experience than Palin. Barack Obama served almost eight years in the Illinois statehouse before his 2004 election to the Senate, where he served an additional two years before beginning his campaign for president. That's a total of ten years in politics before running for president—six fewer than Palin, who was first elected to the Wasilla City Council in 1992. If Palin's lack of experience was such a problem, why wasn't Obama's?

The paradox becomes stranger when you consider what Palin and Obama achieved while in the arena. Palin helped her town grow, hounded out ethical wrongdoers from state politics, cut budgets, and oversaw a major gas line deal. Obama's main accomplishments included delivering an antiwar speech in 2002, a famous call for national unity in 2004, and writing two bestsellers. Time and again, Sarah Palin had made tough calls, challenged authority, and demonstrated true political courage. Barack Obama's career has been an object lesson in political expediency. Prior to his elevation to the presidency, Obama was not known for a single major legislative achievement. In an interview with the obsequiously pro-Obama Chris Matthews, for instance, Obama supporter Kirk Watson could not identify a single legislative accomplishment of Obama's despite repeated opportunities to do so.

Republicans were not the only ones to question Obama's readiness. "I know Senator McCain has a lifetime of experience that he will bring to the White House," Hillary Clinton told reporters in March 2008, then added: "And Senator Obama has a speech he gave in 2002." Bill Clinton called Obama's career a "fairy tale." Joe Biden, Obama's own vice president, said in August 2007 that "I think [Obama] can be ready, but right now I don't believe he is."

This is not to suggest that, at the time of her selection, Palin was more qualified than Obama. Nor is it necessarily true that "experience" should be all that important when electing citizens to high office. The Constitution does not stipulate that an individual must spend a certain amount of time in government before becoming president or vice president. Indeed, the idea that some candidates are better than others by virtue of their résumé corrodes the republican ideal. In our system, all men and women are created equal. All men and women have the right to vote. And all men and women, if they are of age and meet residency requirements, are eligible to hold public office. The point is that the experience argument should have cut against *both* Obama and Palin. Instead, it seemed only to matter with regard to the lady from Alaska.

An August 30, 2008, editorial from the *San Jose Mercury News* suggested why this was so. "Palin may have small-town spunk and kitchen-table common sense," the editors wrote, "but she's patently unqualified for the office." Even though Palin had accomplished more as mayor and governor than Barack Obama had as state senator and senator, the *Mercury News* editorial board said it was "ridiculous" to "argue that Palin is no less experienced than Obama." Why? The reason was that "[i]n the Senate, in organizing a stunningly successful national campaign and through eighteen months of hard campaigning for the nomination, Obama proved to be as capable, articulate, and knowledgeable as anyone in Congress." Translation: They knew Obama. They didn't know

Palin. He was "articulate" and "knowledgeable." She had a funny accent and had never appeared on *Meet the Press*. What more was there to discuss?

In our politics, what one has done matters less than where one has done it. Palin's career took place out of sight, far away in Alaska. The American public first saw Obama during his nationally televised speech at the 2004 Democratic National Convention, and thereafter his visage never left the media eye. His résumé thus carried more weight, because he was the known quantity. The same rule applied to John Edwards, who spent exactly one term in the U.S. Senate before running for president in 2004, losing, joining the Kerry ticket as vice president, losing, then running for president again in 2008 and—surprise—losing. Only rarely, however, does the word "inexperienced" come up when describing Edwards. What's more, one of the top names on Obama's vice presidential shortlist was Virginia governor Tim Kaine. Kaine was elected governor in 2005—just a year before Palin—but it is safe to assume that had he been chosen, he would have been treated more fairly than she. "She hasn't been lectured to by the press for the requisite amount of time," a senior Palin campaign aide said sarcastically.

The Palin-is-unqualified argument was carried to ridiculous extremes. On September 10, Carol Fowler, the chairwoman of the South Carolina Democratic Party, said that Palin's "primary qualification seems to be that she hasn't had an abortion." Fowler later apologized, but her outburst broadcast what was on many liberals' minds. Later, in an October 6, 2008, *Newsweek* column, Fareed Zakaria wrote that "Sarah Palin is utterly unqualified to be vice president." His evidence was that "she has never spent a day thinking about any important national or international issue." Really? Not *one* day? Zakaria's absurd claim—had he read Palin's diary?—is false on its face. And Zakaria would have known so, had he bothered to look at Palin through unbiased eyes. After all, her entire governorship centered on energy and ethics. Aren't those "important national or international" issues?

Saying that Palin was unqualified was the pundits' way of establishing their status as the imperial arbiters of American politics. The pundits' implicit assumption was that the media, not John McCain and certainly not the voters, ought to have final say over who is fit to hold office. And yet the attack on Palin's qualifications was only the start. The real vitriol arrived when the feral beast saw Palin's home—and bared its teeth.

CHAPTER THREE
The Village and the City: There's No Place Like Home

"BETWEEN urban life in the city and provincial life outside the city," Irving Kristol wrote in his essay "Urban Civilization and Its Discontents," "there has always been a gulf of mistrust, suspicion, and contempt." One of the most salient facts about Sarah Palin is that she was born, raised, and has flourished outside the urban metropolises that dominate America's political, financial, and cultural life. As such, she was greeted by the "mistrust, suspicion, and contempt" Kristol so eloquently described.

Although it is true that most Alaskans, like most Americans, live in urban areas, an Alaskan's proximity to the wilderness means that his environment is truly different from that of a suburban or city dweller in the Lower 48. The plants and animals in Alaska are untamed and closer to the people. There are more guns. Escape from others is convenient. And the land is huge. It engulfs and dwarfs you. There is a palpable feeling of closeness to the earth.

This is not the type of place where most Americans live. Nor is it even close to the extremely dense coastal megalopolis that the media and liberal pundits call home. The city is a bustling place, teeming with activity, noise, pollution, congestion, and commerce. In the city, it often seems as though the only wild animals outside the zoo are pigeons, rats, and squirrels. There is more of everything—culture, wealth, goods, people—except unspoiled nature. Alaska and New York City could not be more different.

Behavioral economists like to talk about availability bias, or the human tendency to generalize from recent conditions and present circumstances. Most of us have direct contact with only the small corner of the world we inhabit. We may watch documentaries or read books about other places, but we have no experiential knowledge of them. And while we express solidarity with our fellow countrymen and share a national culture, we also find nonlocal ways of speech and life strange, amusing, and sometimes threatening. Liberals like Barack Obama and Sonia Sotomayor often mention how we are all products of our identity and experience. They have a point. If only liberals would apply the same understanding and tolerance to people who do not share their identities and experiences.

Instead, a gulf of ignorance, misunderstanding, and invective separates the Americans who live in urban areas from the Americans who live in distant provinces and rural places like you'd find in Alaska. One of the few times Barack Obama faltered during the 2008 campaign was when, in the spring, he told attendees at a San Francisco fund-raiser, "You go into some of these small towns in Pennsylvania, and like a lot of small towns in the Midwest, the jobs have been gone now for twenty-five years and nothing's replaced them. And they fell through the Clinton administration, and the Bush administration, and each successive administration has said that somehow these communities are gonna regenerate, and they have not. And it's not surprising, then, they get bitter, they cling to guns or religion or antipathy to people who aren't like them or antiimmigrant sentiment or antitrade sentiment, as a way to explain their frustrations." This was a product of Columbia and Harvard, a professor at the University of Chicago law school, a United States senator who as president would take his wife on "date nights" to New York City, distilling small-town life for an urban audience: guns, God, "antipathy to people who aren't like them," xenophobia, and isolationism. A stark scene.

Not to mention incredibly stereotypical. Clearly parochialism is a two-way street. Yet Obama's description of the provinces was tame compared with some of the invective hurled at Sarah Palin's Alaska. CNN's Jack Cafferty, for example, condescendingly described the last frontier as "a state that has thirteen people and some caribou." *Chicago Sun-Times* columnist Mary Mitchell wrote that Palin came from "the backwoods." On September 4, 2008, John Doyle took to the pages of Canada's *Globe and Mail* to lament that "Alaskan hillbillies have been transplanted into the world of Washington politics." University of Connecticut professor Robert Thorson wrote in the September 11, 2008, *Hartford Courant* that in Wasilla, "[h]igh school sports would substitute for political excitement. Pentecostal and Bible-banging congregations would offer succor, becoming a dominant influence in an isolated town in an isolated state with libertarian leanings and an isolated state capital. This is the kind of geography that scares me."

The idea that the village is a home to dunces ran through the various insults. "Small towns," Canadian writer Heather Mallick pronounced on the *Guardian*'s Web site on September 5, 2008, "are places that smart people escape from, for privacy, for variety, for intellect, for survival. Palin should have stayed home." Mallick, incidentally, grew up in a small town, so "Palin cannot out-hick me."

According to some antiprovincialists, the people who live in small towns are not only stupid but also dangerous. That same month, Connecticut College professor Catherine McNicol Stock wrote in the *Philadelphia Inquirer* that Palin's "beliefs are not just extreme—they are radical, and even bear a comparison with some of the most notorious 'rural radicals' of our time. . . . [W]e should never forget that in the late twentieth century, ultra-Christian, antistatist, and white supremacist groups flourished in the states of the Pacific Northwest—called by many the 'Great White Northwest'—the very region that Sarah Palin and her family call home . . . [T]he beliefs of ultraconservative, evangelical churches like her family's come dangerously close to those of the Christian Identity movement."

McNicol Stock's piece is an amazing work of sophistry posing as considered opinion. There is absolutely nothing in Palin's biography or politics that suggests any relationship with the Christian Identity movement or far-right domestic terrorism. Obama, meanwhile, had a personal relationship with a former left-wing terrorist, Bill Ayers, for more than a decade. When Palin mentioned this association on the stump, however, the media criticized her, saying she had stepped over the line that separates polite discourse from demagogy.

WHERE SHE IS FROM

For the media types who reside in America's major cities, all of their fellow citizens—whether they live on a farm or in a small town, a suburb, an exurb, or even a midsize city like, say, Omaha—are of lesser status. The media distinguish only between sophisticated metropolitan culture and everything else. They pay no mind to the diverse communities across America. Such bias blinded liberals to one of Palin's major accomplishments. As mayor of Wasilla, she had presided over the town's transition from rural backwater to thriving suburb. Rather than take an objective view of the town where she grew up, rather than acknowledge how she had helped her village flourish, pundits were content to minimize Palin as an unsophisticated outsider.

Wasilla is an accident. The town incorporated in 1917, but its population hardly grew beyond a couple hundred people until the Great Depression. In the mid-1930s, FDR decided to implement a rural rehabilitation program in the Mat-Su Valley. The feds brought up around two hundred farmers from the northern parts of Minnesota and Wisconsin to till the soil and grow crops. The project was a bust. Seventy-five of the original families left within a year.

The colony was saved in 1940 when the government decided to remilitarize Alaska. The threat of war created jobs for the people left in the valley. They would take the train into Anchorage to build the Fort Richardson and Elmendorf military bases. After the bases were built, there were jobs with the companies that catered to the soldiers. The Mat-Su Valley had plenty of cheap real estate and proximity to the largest city in the state. But it was far enough from Anchorage for the Mat-Su colonists to live out their fantasy of frontier life, after work and on the weekends.

"Wasilla is an unusual piece of Alaska," Stephen Haycox, a historian at the University of Alaska Anchorage, told me. "People move out there who are *more* impatient with government regulation than the average Alaskan." And the average Alaskan is already pretty impatient with government regulation. The families who reside in the Mat-Su Valley are "willing to drive to Anchorage for work, cultural outlets, and amenities," Haycox said, "because living in Wasilla allows them to live out the rhetorical ideal of Alaskan life."

In the early 1990s, "Wasilla was a lawless place," Nick Carney said in an interview. Carney lives in Utah now, but for years he lived in

Wasilla, where he sat on the city council and ran the local waste management company. Carney worked closely with Wasilla's mayor in the early 1990s, a soft-spoken man named John Stein. To confront the burglaries and drug use plaguing Wasilla, Stein proposed a 2 percent sales tax to pay for a local police force. The proposal encountered considerable opposition. Stein's task was to convince the public that a low sales tax would take Wasilla to the next level of development.

For that, Stein needed to find new voices that could appeal to different constituencies. He turned to councilman Carney, who began a search. "We were looking for someone to represent the younger voters in the city to support the police force," Carney explained. Someone mentioned Sarah Palin. Carney and Stein contacted Palin and asked if she'd be interested in speaking on behalf of the sales tax and police force, and also in running for the Wasilla City Council. Palin said she was.

On Election Day 1992 the voters approved the sales tax, and Sarah Palin won a seat on the city council. A first time officeholder, she kept a low profile. "The first couple of years," Carney said, "she did what we expected her to do and hoped she would do." John Stein had the same recollection. "She was always there," he told me. "I don't think she ever offered anything as her own initiative. Nothing really came from her. We didn't see much initiative coming out of her. I was used to more active participants." Active or not, the voters were happy. Palin was reelected to a second term in 1994.

Carney and Stein had recruited Palin into municipal politics, but she was no rubber stamp. A rule in politics is to "dance with the one who brung ya." Palin has never followed this rule. For example, when Wasilla was about to enter a contract with Carney's waste management company to haul residents' garbage, Palin pounced. The contract would have given Carney's company a monopoly. But people should have the choice to haul their junk to the dump if they want, Palin said. She voted no on the resolution.

Palin's criticisms of Stein and Carney grew in intensity. She supported the sales tax but said Stein was putting the revenues the tax had generated to poor use. In her view, Stein was a big spender. Carney distinctly remembered one council meeting when Palin attacked Stein again and again. He said she kept hitting the spending issue and saying that the Stein budgets were too big, too wasteful. He said she made caustic remarks. He said she rolled her eyes when Stein offered a rebuttal. After the meeting, Carney approached Palin. *You sound like you're running for mayor,* he said.

Carney told me that Palin got upset. *What do you mean?* she asked. All she had been doing was pointing out the flaws in Stein's approach. She had no ambitions for higher office.

A few months later, Palin filed to run for mayor.

What makes a talented politician is the ability to detect changes in the political winds before anyone else. Palin has the knack. For decades, Wasilla had been a small town that had little to do with state or national politics. The focus had been on building infrastructure and delivering services (police, trash pickup, water, and sewer). But Wasilla was transitioning, with more contentious politics and a definite conservative streak. And all this was happening as Palin transitioned from full-time mom to councilwoman to candidate for mayor. Wasilla and Sarah Palin were on parallel tracks.

Palin's opponent Stein, the three-term incumbent, thought of himself as a nonpartisan municipal administrator. That was the way he had governed, the way he wanted to keep governing. But revolutions were brewing in the Lower 48, where President Clinton's follies had brought into existence a coalition of taxpayers, gun owners, religious conservatives, and businesspeople who all wanted the government to let them be. Historically, social values politics had not mattered much in Alaska. But that, too, was about to change. Palin saw what conservative Republicans were doing thousands of miles away and embraced it. The gun owners, taxpayers, and churchgoers would carry her to the mayoralty. It was the cunning of history. Stein didn't have a chance.

At the time, John Stein was a registered Republican, but he had neither campaigned nor governed in an ideological fashion. (He told me he has always been more liberal than conservative.) Stein lacked a partisan profile, which is a sure road to defeat in an election fought on partisan grounds. Palin's genius was to transform a sleepy municipal election into a philosophical grudge match. Stein was not conservative enough for the Mat-Su Valley, Palin charged. She pointed out that he was pro-choice, whereas Palin was unabashedly pro-life. Stein had joined the NRA only in the run-up to the campaign and opposed a conceal-carry law, whereas Palin was a lifetime NRA member who opposed most gun controls. Stein said that he had spent city revenue to build infrastructure, whereas Palin said he was being wasteful and kept the overall municipal tax burden too high.

Palin's insurgent mayoral campaign was fought over three issues—guns, spending, and abortion—which helped her build a winning majority. This was savvy politics for a thirty-two-year-old mom who had no political background and no ties to the establishment. Wasilla voters elected her overwhelmingly in October 1996, 60 percent to 40 percent.

The new mayor had run on a platform of smaller government and fewer taxes, and that was what she gave her city. She reduced the budget. She cut the mayor's salary. She left the sales tax alone, but reduced property and business inventory taxes. Then she delivered on a bond issue to improve local infrastructure.

Palin's first term was a success. The clearest evidence of this was that no one was eager to challenge her for reelection. When Mayor Palin's term was up in 1999, her opponent—once again—was John Stein. "Nobody else was challenging her," he told me. "And I felt this duty to get out there and call people's attention to what was going on. Ideology had trumped practicality."

The voters disagreed. Palin trounced Stein in the October 1999 election, taking 76 percent of the vote.

Palin's agenda had been clear when she first ran for mayor in 1996, but she stood for reelection without a laundry list of policy proposals. She wanted to continue to oversee Wasilla's growth and ensure that the public sector did not hamper the private economy. But her eye was also on higher office, and a second term would build her résumé.

Since the major infrastructure had already been completed, city politics increasingly centered on quality of life. Residents wanted to improve and expand the public facilities available to them. Palin convinced the voters to accept a half-point increase in the sales tax and another bond issue in order to build a sports arena and recreation center. There was only one problem. The city did not own the site where it wanted to build. Palin entered into a protracted legal fight over the land purchase that, as of this writing, still is not fully resolved. Nevertheless, the Curtis D. Menard Memorial Sports Center—featuring a hockey rink, a turf court, a running track, and meeting rooms—was built. Palin achieved her goal. Even her critics acknowledge that the arena fight was a challenge. "It was only her personal magnetism" that got it built, Nick Carney said.

In 2009 Nick Carney published a book, *Our Home Is Wasilla.* "Wasilla now has Wal-Mart, Lowe's, Home Depot, Fred Meyers, Target, car dealerships, too many rather ugly strip malls with all manner of shops, restaurants, more fast food stores than restaurants, stoplights, sewage and water systems, storage units, parks, police and fire protection, new schools, traffic, and congestion," Carney wrote. "Some of the bars and all the churches are still there, nearly lost in the shuffle. One no longer has to go to Anchorage to shop. It has lost its small town atmosphere, inevitable, I suppose, in the face of the immense growth of the area since. No one has yet found a way for areas to grow and not change, nor could you expect that to happen in Wasilla."

"A monkey could've run the city of Wasilla," a local small-business woman told me. But that is not quite true. A less talented politician, or one opposed to development, could have stalled Wasilla's growth. It was Palin who supervised Wasilla's transformation from nowheresville to active suburb. It was Palin who catalyzed the expansion and maturation of her town. Such a transformation may offend antisprawl liberals, but what of it? The Mat-Su Valley continues to be the fastest-growing area in Alaska. People keep coming in. They want to live there. They like it.

Anti-Antiprovincialism

When you visit Wasilla, you see a lot of strip malls, cars, churches, and small businesses. The big news in Wasilla is the opening of the latest big-box retail franchise. The folks who live there shop at Wal-Mart or consignment stores. They live a different sort of life than the new media professional who shares a third-floor walk-up in Brooklyn and takes the subway to work in the morning. "Fine dining" in Wasilla is the Glacier Canyon Grill. The town museum could fit inside a Hummer. The range of experience is comparatively limited. The population is less ethnically diverse.

Plenty of Americans live in such a manner. Yet the antiprovincial liberal looks down on these Americans as backward. The antiprovincial liberal sees his fellow Americans who live in a place like Wasilla as lacking the sophistication necessary to manipulate the American economy through public policy. The antiprovincial liberal sees his fellow Americans as subjects, not citizens.

There is a long tradition of antiprovincial thought in European and American intellectual life. This line of thinking is as old as the divide between city and country. The Irving Kristol essay quoted above, which captures the tension between the village and the city better than most everything else, was written in 1970—just a few years after Sarah Palin was born. It is not news that city dwellers look down on the men and women who live in (or hail from) the sticks. Nor is it shocking that provincials view metropolitans as prissy, spoiled, decadent elitists. What is remarkable, though, is that liberals expend so much effort studying, thinking about, analyzing, and identifying with the Other, yet they rarely treat the Other in their midst—whether regional or political—with the same respect they give to disadvantaged groups with historical grievances around the globe. The farmer in Chiapas is worthy of pity and aid. But the farmer in rural Kansas is worthy of fear and condescension.

Consider the unwarranted assumptions, lazy generalizations, caricature, and stereotype contained in the following September 8, 2008, blog entry on the *Huffington Post.* "In [Palin's] world and the world of Fundamentalists," the author wrote, "nothing changes or gets better or evolves. [Palin] does not believe in global warming. The melting of the Arctic, the storms that are destroying our cities, the pollution and rise of cancers, are all parts of God's plan. She is fighting to take the polar bears off the endangered species list. The earth, in Palin's view, is here to be taken and plundered. The wolves and the bears are here to be shot and plundered. The oil is here to be taken and plundered . . . Sarah Palin does not much believe in thinking. From what I gather she has tried to ban books from the library, has a tendency to dispense with people who think independently. She cannot tolerate an environment of ambiguity and difference . . . Sarah believes in guns. She has her own custom Austrian hunting rifle. She has been known to kill forty caribou at a clip. She has shot hundreds of wolves from the air . . . If the polar bears don't move you to go and do everything in your power to get Obama elected, then consider" Palin's support for oil drilling. "I think of teeth when I think of drills," the author continued. "I think of rape. I think of destruction. I think of domination. I think of military exercises that force mindless repetition, emptying the brain of analysis, doubt, ambiguity or dissent. I think of pain."

The real pain comes from reading such tripe. The author of this passage is Eve Ensler, the celebrated feminist activist and author of *The Vagina Monologues*. Her take on Palin is riddled with factual errors and nonsensical exaggerations, but it also exemplifies the paranoia and loathing that some on the left exhibit toward the denizens of America's rural areas, small towns, and suburbs. Ensler's mistaken beliefs and prejudices are widely shared. When I printed out this blog post in April 2009, there were 554 comments appended to it. The comments were overwhelmingly positive. Clearly Ensler had hit a nerve—an ugly one.

Diversity is a liberal virtue. It is something to be cherished. Yet all too often writers favor one way of life, the city or the country, over the other. In the liberal imagination, the city is the vanguard of modernity and cosmopolitanism. The country is a historical relic. "The ordinariness, and randomness, and, even, perfidiousness, of small-town American life," author Michael Wolff wrote on his blog, Off the Grid, on March 12, 2009, "is the Palin story." Sarah Palin's Alaska, Joe Klein wrote in a column published on Time.com on September 10, 2008, "represents the last, lingering hint of that most basic Huckleberry Finn fantasy—lighting out for the territories." Emphasis on the "fantasy" part: Klein's article was titled "Sarah Palin's Myth of America." "We haven't been a nation of small towns for nearly a century," Klein wrote. "It is the suburbanites and city dwellers who do the fighting and hourly-wage work now, and the corporations who grow our food." Support for Palin, Klein argued, was nothing more than an exercise in nostalgia, an irrational, last-ditch attempt to recover the "Main Street that existed before America began losing wars, became ostentatiously sexy and casually interracial." According to Klein, Sarah Palin's America is a place "not unlike C. Vann Woodward's South, where myths are more potent than the hope of getting past the dour realities [Americans] face each day."

The reference to Southern historian C. Vann Woodward is illuminating. Klein has no other point of comparison. For him, Wasilla, Alaska—a bustling exurb thousands of miles away from Mobile, Alabama—most closely resembles the Jim Crow South. Klein is incapable of describing Wasilla in its own terms, of situating it in a national context of suburban growth and sprawl. To do so, one supposes, would be to suggest that Wasilla isn't so strange and dangerous a place after all.

America is a big, roiling, burgeoning, varied country that has plenty of room for small towns and big cities alike. Each locale has its pluses and minuses. None is better than the other. True diversity allows space for each.

We all suffer from availability bias. But the media especially ought to guard against it, since their job is to transmit information in the most unbiased manner possible. In Palin's case, however, the media's unstated assumptions about her background all too often added a patronizing tone to their coverage. "What newspapers and magazines did you regularly read before you were tapped for this to stay informed and to understand the world?" Katie Couric asked Palin, as though the governor was Nanook of the North Pole, a primitive cut off from civilization. No wonder Palin's answer was evasive. She was angry at Couric, she explained later to *Media Malpractice* director John Ziegler, for implying that it wasn't normal for people in Alaska to read papers and keep in touch with the events of the day. Of course Palin reads newspapers. She regularly reads *USA Today,* the *Anchorage Daily News,* and the *Mat-Su Valley Frontiersman.* As a politician, she needs to follow the news. She has written numerous op-ed articles and letters to the editor. She has provided countless interviews and quotes.

Antiprovincialism is not limited to lefties. Some of Palin's campaign handlers also saw her as an alien interloper who was more fit for a menagerie of American life than the West Wing. One McCain aide told me that the Palins had no idea "how things were done" in a major presidential campaign. The reason? On the day of the governor's debut, on the bus, the aide said that Todd Palin handed the governor a phone and told her, *Here, talk to these people.* On the other end of the line were the hosts of a call-in radio show in Alaska. The interview was spur of the moment and hadn't been cleared by McCain's press office.

One interpretation of the incident would be to say it proves that the Palins were a breath of fresh air. Another interpretation, the one adopted by many of the political professionals on the campaign, was that McCain had brought an amateur on board. A senior McCain adviser told me that whenever Palin had a snafu, her handlers would roll their eyes and say, "All roads go back to Wasilla."

"There was a culture gap," the senior adviser said. Top campaign brass saddled Palin with aides who "wouldn't be caught dead in a Wal-Mart. They just couldn't believe people would shoot a moose or take their kids to salmon fishing camp for a month."

Many people do exactly that, however. Which helps explain Palin's appeal and magnifies the confusion of her detractors. The coastal establishment couldn't comprehend this upstart. Nor could much of the McCain campaign. Palin was alone. She was caught in the empty space between the village and the city.

CHAPTER FOUR
The Ties That Bind: The Blistering Assault on Palin's Family

A new issue of *US Weekly* hit the newsstands on September 2, days after Sarah Palin's debut. Typically, the glossy celebrity magazine is stuffed with pictures of the latest "it" girls and page after slickly printed page of actresses' diet plans, shopping routines, summer flings, and tan lines. The copy is written at something akin to a fourth-grade reading level. The magazine's content is so light, it practically floats off the ground.

The September 2 issue made a play for weightier matters, however. The cover model was neither Lindsay Lohan nor Britney Spears. It was Sarah Palin. And though Palin's looks certainly passed magazine-model muster, her hairdo and designer glasses did not concern the editors at *US Weekly.* Their project was to suggest that Palin's family life was as tumultuous and scandal-ridden as that of the latest Hollywood ingenue. "John McCain's Vice President Sarah Palin: Babies, Lies & Scandal," the headline read. The cover teased that Palin, "under attack, admits daughter, seventeen, is pregnant." Another tagline screamed that Palin was being "investigated for firing of sister's ex-husband!" The third cover line: "Mom of five: New embarrassing surprises."

US Weekly's owner, media magnate Jann Wenner, was an Obama donor and outspoken Democrat. The cover story, "Sarah Palin: Political Opponent Recalls Being Ridiculed," did not disclose this conflict of interest. What it did do, however, was quote Lyda Green extensively (she had opposed the governor in the Alaska state legislature) and the Berkeley professor and liberal writer George Lakoff. A balanced report it was not.

What made the *US Weekly* issue notable was not its one-sidedness, hype, and partisanship. You could read Palin's coverage in the *New York Times* and find similar tendentiousness and mendacity. The attention that the celebrity magazine lavished on Palin was significant for different reasons. One was that the cover heralded Palin's transition from mere politician to global celebrity. She was no longer the lady from Wasilla who took on the establishment and brought power back to the Alaskan people. She was . . . *Sarah! Palin!* . . . a figure whose persona extended beyond the realm of mere politics and captured the imagination of millions of people who rarely gave a second thought to public affairs.

The *US Weekly* story was important for another reason, too. It was the opening salvo in a full-scale attempt to turn Palin into a dangerous and irresponsible woman. Other tabloids also promoted this narrative. The *National Enquirer*'s headline read SARAH PALIN'S DARK SECRETS! *People* magazine announced, "Sarah Palin's Family Drama." The objective was to distort the public image of Palin, the young mother of five who seemed to balance work and family without batting an eyelash.

The McCain campaign had always wanted to showcase Palin's large family. The campaign understood her clan's broad appeal. Images of

Palin, her husband, and their two sons and three daughters were power-ful reminders that the governor celebrated the values of hard work and family. Snapshots of Palin holding her son Trig also reminded conserva-tive activists that Palin not only believed in the right to life, she prac-ticed it. "The family was part of the package," Michael Goldfarb told me. "That was part of the deal."

I have talked to a lot of folks who have spent time around the Palins, including even a former babysitter, and they all told me how impressed they were by the family's closeness and normalcy. They described Sarah and Todd Palin as engaged and energetic parents. Lindsay Hayes, for example, worked on Palin's speechwriting team. She recalled a staff visit to Alaska with the governor shortly after the convention. "The Palins are an impressive family," Hayes told me. "They're in this together. Every-one pitches in. And I was struck by how effortless the governor made it look—she seemed to move so easily through all these things. It was clear that this was who she is."

A senior Palin campaign aide who spent hours on the trail with the governor agreed. Palin had a "phenomenal relationship with her chil-dren and husband," the aide said. "The family was close. They moved around with such ease together. She was attentive to her familial respon-sibilities in a manner that didn't subtract from her duties as a candidate. Was she distracted? No. She was keeping a balance in her life. Using the word 'distracted' is the perspective of people who don't have a family."

It was amazing, though, the number of folks who had never met the Palins but felt themselves qualified to remark on the family's most intimate secrets. Over the course of Sarah Palin's first weeks in the pub-lic eye, the spurious revelations and false accusations were unremitting. Palin's political opponents charged that she had abused her office to protect her family. Tabloids said Palin's marriage was on the rocks. Blog-gers questioned the maternity of her youngest child. Pundits accused

Palin of bad parenting. Rumormongers spread the idea that her older son was a delinquent. A voter who casually glanced at magazine headlines while standing in the supermarket checkout line must have thought that Palin was some strange combination of Dina Lohan and Joan Crawford.

It was all lies.

Talking about the media's double standard is at this point like saying the sky is blue. It's a law of nature: the media are more likely to cover Democrats in a positive light than Republicans. But there's another aspect to the double standard: the media are also more likely to respect the privacy of Democrats than of Republicans. The media wouldn't touch the story when Al Gore's son was arrested on drug charges in 2003 and 2007. Nor should they have done so. This was a family matter for the Gores, and the media held their fire. Yet every time one of the Bush daughters was caught breaking the rules governing alcohol consumption, the matter became a topic of national import.

For months, the mainstream media would not touch the John Edwards affair story with a ten-foot pole, even as the *National Enquirer* published detail after detail regarding the former Democratic vice presidential nominee's relationship with onetime campaign staffer Rielle Hunter. Yet in February 2008, apropos of nothing, the *New York Times* published three thousand words on John McCain's friendship with a female lobbyist. The meandering article stopped short of accusing McCain of infidelity, but that was its clear implication. A year later, the *Times* issued a statement: "The *Times* did not intend to conclude that [the lobbyist] had engaged in a romantic affair with Senator McCain or an unethical relationship on behalf of her clients in breach of the public trust." Good to know. By that time, however, the damage was done.

When Obama said in June 2008 that "I think families are off-limits," the media bowed and scraped as usual. Thereafter, the press disqualified criticism of Michelle Obama. As well they should have done; the candidate is the person on the ballot and therefore the one who should be exposed to inquiry and criticism. Families really ought to be off-limits. But apparently the press thought Obama meant only *Democratic* families. Because as late as September 2008, the *Washington Post* published a hit job on Cindy McCain, titled "A Tangled Story of Addiction." And in October 2008, the *New York Times* also published an article on Cindy McCain that said she had been "a liability at times" for her husband. All families are off-limits, but some families are more off-limits than others.

With the Palins, the limits disappeared entirely. Since the media had not heard of Palin, they were inclined to pore over every last personal and biographical detail in an attempt to understand her. The problem with this approach was that it allowed errors, exaggerations, and mis-characterizations to seep into the reporting. Meanwhile, Democrats and liberal hacks in print, radio, television, and cyberspace declared open season on Palin's family without regard to the consequences.

On September 4, on Slate.com, Hanna Rosin offhandedly referred to Palin's "wreck of a home life." On September 9, scholar Wendy Doniger, a contributor to the Washington Post Company's On Faith blog, lectured Palin: "Don't humiliate members of your family in order to get elected to public office." On September 10, in the *Nation,* Katha Pollitt wrote about the "wacky carnival on ice that is the Palin family." And in a September 12 "Diary" on Daily Kos, the failed Democratic congressional candidate Paul Hackett urged his copartisans to run the following hateful, error-filled ad against McCain-Palin: "Sarah Palin? Can't keep her solemn oath of devotion to her husband and had sex with his employee. Sarah Palin? Accidentally got pregnant at age forty-three and the tax payers of Alaska have to pay for the care of her disabled child. Sarah Palin? Unable to teach her sixteen-year-old daughter right from wrong and now another teenager is pregnant. Sarah Palin? Can you trust Sarah Palin and her values with America's future?"

The Democrats and their allies said that the Palin family was "fair game" because the governor had made her sons and daughters part of her life story. What did Palin's opponents expect her to do? *Not* mention her family? Every politician with a nice family highlights that element of their personality. It humanizes them and brings them down to earth. Obama, for instance, had his children talk to a national audience on *Access Hollywood.* Nobody attacked or joked about Malia and Sasha. There was no reason to. Doing so would have crossed the line. And yet the Palin children are ridiculed and slandered to this day.

There is no question that campaign disorder and confusion, the monumental task of getting up-to-speed on a politician hardly anybody in the Lower 48 had ever heard of, contributed a lot to the shoddy treatment of Palin's family. And yet the slurs cannot be excused in such a manner. They were part of a political project. As soon as Sarah Palin was nominated, Democrats and their helpers embarked on a monumental quest to turn her into something she was not, whether that was a typical pol, a neglectful mom, a religious zealot, or a bimbo. Puncturing the idea that Palin's big family was happy and content was a start.

Liberals, Goldfarb said, "think we're all hypocrites. They think every Republican is a David Vitter hypocrite [Vitter, a socially conservative senator from Louisiana, admitted in 2007 to soliciting prostitutes]. But she isn't. She's the real thing. She doesn't go hunting like Kerry did for the campaign; she field-dresses a moose like it's nothing. It was the first time Obama wasn't the lead story, and Biden's plane was empty [of political reporters]! So they had to make her out to be a hypocrite. And how do you do that? Make her out to be a bad mother."

Storm Troopers

Mike Wooten was trouble. The Alaska state trooper was the ex-husband of Palin's younger sister, Molly. The separation had not been amicable. Wooten had a history of misbehavior. He drank to excess, had illegally killed a cow-moose without a license, and had used a Taser on his eleven-year-old stepson. The Palin family alleged that Wooten had harassed Molly and her father, Chuck Heath, since the divorce.

"Wooten does not tell the truth," Sarah Palin wrote to Colonel Julia Grimes of the Alaska Department of Public Safety on August 10, 2005. "He intimidates people and abuses his position. I don't know what more can be said, except that considering just a few examples from those I've shared with you (namely, the death threat against my father who is merely trying to help his daughter escape a horribly abusive relationship, the illegal hunting, and the drunk driving!) all would lead a rational person to believe there is a problem inside the organization."

It's up to private citizens—whom Palin was when she wrote Colonel Grimes—to lodge complaints and pressure the Alaska Department of Public Safety for action. The entire Palin family was concerned about Wooten. To them, he was a bad seed who threatened not only his ex-wife and her relatives but also the Alaskan populace at large. Moreover, his continued employment as a trooper marred the state law-enforcement department's public image. "For police officers to violate the public trust is a grave, grave violation—in my opinion," Governor Palin wrote to Walt Monegan, her commissioner of public safety, on February 7, 2007. "We have too many examples lately of cops and troopers who violate the public trust and DPS has come across as merely turning a blind eye or protecting that officer, seemingly 'for the good of the brotherhood.' "

Palin felt strongly about a particular example. Wooten, she continued, "is still out on the street, in fact he's been promoted. It was a joke, the whole year-long 'investigation' of him—in fact those who passed along the serious information about him to Julia Grimes and [former public safety commissioner Bill] Tandeske were threatened with legal action from the trooper's union for speaking about it. (This is the same trooper who's out there today telling people the new administration is going to destroy the trooper organization, and that he'd 'never work for that b*tch, Palin'.)"

Palin had a tendency to bring up Wooten whenever she heard reports about malfeasant troopers. On May 5, 2007, Palin's chief of staff, Mike Tibbles, sent her a report alleging that a trooper in Fairbanks had sexually assaulted a minor. Palin copied Monegan on her response. "[W]ell Mike," she wrote, "between this and the message I received the other night where an AK State Trooper recently told a friend of the family that he could further 'mess with the governor's sister' by claiming falsehoods about us—well—some of our 'finest' in uniform continue to disappoint." In another e-mail to Monegan, regarding a gun-control proposal, Palin wrote: "The first thought that hit me when reading Gara's quote about people not being able to buy guns when they're threatening to kill someone went to my ex brother-in-law, the trooper, who threatened to kill my dad yet was not even reprimanded by his bosses and still to this day carries a gun, of course. We can't have double standards."

Nowhere in these e-mails did Palin instruct Monegan to terminate Wooten's employment. In fact, there is absolutely no evidence that Palin ever told anyone to fire Wooten. More than a year later, however, when Palin fired Monegan on July 11, 2008, the disgruntled former employee wasted no time linking his dismissal to the wayward trooper. The political firestorm that resulted quickly became known as "Troopergate."

At issue: Did Sarah and Todd Palin pressure Monegan to fire Wooten? And if so, did this constitute a violation of the state ethics law?

The phony scandal was the first time when Palin's family life became politicized and subject to close scrutiny. Troopergate was a political hot potato in the middle of a presidential election, and it was an object lesson in the insidious dangers of using ethics statutes to ensnare political opponents in legal traps. For Palin's adversaries in Alaska, Troopergate was a cudgel with which they could strike her. Their aim was to criminalize policy differences and personal enmity.

Monegan is a talented bureaucratic operator. He had friends in the legislature, including Hollis French, the powerful Alaska state senator. French quickly organized an investigation into Palin that was sure to distract her from pursuing her agenda. The issue broke during the summer, when the legislature wasn't in session. For that reason French turned to the Legislative Council, a smaller body devoted to conducting state business during recess. On July 28, the Legislative Council voted 12 to 0 to hire a special prosecutor to investigate any wrongdoing. The council chose Stephen Branchflower, a retired Anchorage prosecutor and friend of Monegan's, to lead the inquiry. But everybody knew French was in charge.

The Legislative Council was stacked with Republicans. The vote to investigate was bipartisan. Palin's critics in the Lower 48 used these facts to suggest that the council's inquisition was with merit. It was not. The critics conveniently forgot that plenty of Palin's enemies in Alaska are Republicans.

Branchflower had two limitations: an artificial deadline and the inability to subpoena anyone he wanted. But these were minor hurdles. The goal from the start was to target Palin, whose nomination to the vice presidency only made the investigation's outcome more important.

The Legislative Council ensured that Branchflower would issue his report prior to Election Day, in the hopes that it would inflict the maximum possible amount of political damage. Hollis French made comments to the effect that Branchflower's findings would be an "October surprise." Members of the legislature say that the majority leader of the state senate coalition at the time, Johnny Ellis, had a separate BlackBerry devoted to communications with the Obama campaign. "It was more theater than about searching out the truth," former state senator Gene Therriault told me.

The upside for Palin was that her newfound prominence gave her a strong legal defense team. The McCain campaign's top echelon knew about Troopergate when Palin was put on the ticket. As soon as she debuted, then, the campaign dispatched lawyers to Alaska to assist the governor's personal counsel. The Washington lawyers were dismayed at what they found on the last frontier. "One of the first things we concluded was that the outcome of the Branchflower investigation had been predetermined," a member of the vetting team who was on the ground in Alaska told me.

The best option, therefore, was to go to the Personnel Board. It was the appropriate venue for ethics complaints. Palin had used the board before, when she and Eric Croft went after Attorney General Gregg Renkes. Indeed, the on-the-ground attorney said, when the Legislative Council began its investigation, that Palin should have said that the Personnel Board was the sole appropriate venue for such an inquiry. She did not. And the situation spun out of control.

Palin referred herself to the Personnel Board on September 1, 2008. Meanwhile, in early September, a Republican state legislator named John Coghill requested that the Legislative Council remove French from a supervisory role over Branchflower. Democratic state senator Kim Elton, an Obama supporter and future Obama administration appointee, denied Coghill's request. Both investigations would proceed unfettered. And since Palin and her allies expected that Branchflower would catch her in some error, no matter how trivial, the Personnel Board report was her only real hope for a fair acquittal in the court of public opinion.

It was true that Palin had mentioned Wooten obliquely in several e-mails to Monegan. It was also true that Todd Palin had made frequent complaints to Monegan and others in the department about Wooten's conduct. But these references and complaints had ended long before Monegan got the boot. The last mention of Wooten in a Palin e-mail to Monegan occurred in summer 2007. The last contact between Todd Palin and Monegan was in late 2007. Monegan told the *Anchorage Daily News* on August 30, 2008, that Palin had never asked him to fire Wooten. But he alleged that Palin brought up Wooten during a private phone call and a one-on-one meeting. Palin denied both conversations took place.

But even if these conversations *did* take place—even if, though there is nothing to suggest as much, Palin specifically asked Monegan to fire Wooten—it is hard to argue that she violated ethical protocol. After all, Wooten really was a hazard. The evidence here is not in dispute. The logic of Palin's opponents was faulty. It cannot be the case that just because Sarah Palin is governor, her family must be exposed to the threat of domestic violence without any recourse. Moreover, there is nothing that says a governor, who is charged with securing the public safety, cannot rely on her personal experiences or intimate knowledge of a potential threat to public safety in the execution of her duties. "[E]ven where there is a personal interest in a matter," the Personnel Board later concluded, "there is no violation of the Ethics Act if the action taken by the official is to effect an interest that is held by the public or a large class of persons to which the official belongs."

Surely removing from duty a state trooper who is a threat to others is "an interest that is held by the public."

Palin fired Walt Monegan because he had become more of a burden than an asset. The documentary evidence, unearthed in the Personnel Board inquiry, revealed serious disagreements over budgetary matters between Monegan and Palin's senior staff. Over time the discord grew in intensity. At the beginning of the summer of 2008, Monegan scheduled a trip to Washington, D.C., to lobby for money that the governor had cut from the budget. That was when Palin's staff began to discuss how best to fire him.

"She was not involved in the back-and-forth," the on-the-ground member of the vetting team told me. "What was clear," the vetting team member went on, "was that, on the one hand, Wooten really was a rogue actor. But the governor had really compartmentalized the issue. We got the impression that Wooten's name wasn't even mentioned by her after early 2007."

Monegan was a talented civil servant, so Palin offered him another position. He refused, initiating the chain of events that would slow down government, waste taxpayer money, and stress out well-meaning staffers who had to lawyer up and confront the vipers in the state legislature. All to paint a false portrait of Sarah Palin as conniving, petty, and corrupt. "For all the focus on the governor's role," said the vetting team member, "no one has ever denied the underlying facts or explained why it was desirable to have someone like Mike Wooten on the state payroll. And it's ironic that the only reason he remains on the payroll today is that he was lucky enough to be related to the Palin family."

Branchflower issued his findings on October 10, 2008, a little more than three weeks before Election Day. He found that Palin was totally within her rights to fire Monegan. But that was not the conclusion that Obama's allies in Alaska wanted to hear. So Branchflower also found that Palin had violated the state ethics law by not limiting Todd Palin's contacts with Monegan and other officials. "It was just politics right from the get-go," Therriault said. "They got the headline they wanted: 'Governor in Violation of Ethics Statute.'"

Except that the Personnel Board concluded that she was not. It released its report, "[b]ased upon substantially more evidence than was available to Mr. Branchflower," on November 3, 2008, the day before the election. But it was too late. Branchflower's erroneous conclusion had been given weeks to sink in. The most negative reading possible of his findings—that Palin somehow violated the law by failing to control her husband—was another tributary to the river of Palin attacks. Had there been more time, the American public might have been able to understand the Personnel Board report for the total exoneration it was.

The board had deposed Palin for more than three hours. Todd Palin was deposed, too. The final report dismissed all the charges against the governor, saying that "[t]here is no probable cause to believe that Governor Palin violated the Alaska Executive Ethics Act" with her dismissal of Monegan or her handling of the Wooten matter. The Personnel Board counsel found, moreover, that "the wrong statute was used as a basis for the conclusions contained in the Branchflower report, [and] the Branchflower report misconstrued the available evidence and did not consider or obtain all of the material evidence that is required to properly reach findings in this matter."

The Personnel Board went directly after Branchflower's legal reasoning. "If the Branchflower Report's expansive construction of the term 'inaction' were adopted," the board's counsel wrote, "a public official could be sanctioned or punished for failing to take action to prevent persons outside state government from taking action who are not even covered by the Act." And that would be absurd. Furthermore, "No specific evidence was cited in the Branchflower Report about what

Governor Palin knew about the acts of others." Palin began sharing her concerns about Wooten to the state troopers in 2005, when she held no state office and thus was not covered under the Ethics Act. At all times, her husband was an autonomous private citizen whose complaints about a possible security threat to his family took place outside the governor's purview. The whole rigmarole was silly in any case, because the fundamental reality was that the Palins were trying to cope with a man alleged to be a heavy and angry drinker who was comfortable Tasering preteens. What would *anybody* do when confronted with a similar situation?

The Personnel Board's findings were not inevitable. Frank Murkowski had appointed all but one of its members, and the legislature had confirmed all of them. The Murkowski appointees owed Palin nothing. Politics tainted the Legislative Council and the Branchflower report, but it would be a stretch to make the same argument about the Personnel Board. In the end, Palin was vindicated. Her enemies were not. They would have been embarrassed—if they'd had any shame.

WHAT SECRETS LIE IN THE HEARTS OF MEN?

There is a deep-seated tendency among Sarah Palin's opponents to impute to her the worst motives and darkest behaviors. Partly this is because Palin was a stranger from the strangest part of America. You can make a case that people are more willing to entertain bizarre, untrue, and vile notions about Palin because they know so little about her. But that does not fully explain the phenomenon, because many of the worst falsehoods cast against the governor come from those who know her best: Alaskans in general and Wasillans in particular. When Palin became the most famous Republican woman in the world, the Alaskan Palin-haters met willing accomplices in the global media. The rumors, misconceptions, and lies that had spent years festering in the cold could finally bloom in warmer climes.

The Palin conspiracy theorists went after her marriage. To the kooks, Todd Palin is either the brains behind the operation or a loose cannon who threatens Sarah Palin's future. They can't decide which. Both Palins, the nuts say, have had affairs—another baseless accusation. But, on September 3, 2008, the untruth made the news. That week's *National Enquirer*'s cover story, "Sarah Palin's Dark Secrets!" alleged that the governor had had an affair with Todd Palin's former business partner. And ever since the *Enquirer* had been right about John Edwards's infidelity, mainstream reporters were paying attention to the tabloid. The McCain campaign publicly rejected the article's premise and threatened legal action. Inside the campaign, however, there was more trepidation. "At that point, you were just waiting for the other shoe to drop," Goldfarb said. "Nobody anticipated this level of scrutiny."

The story briefly got legs when the former business partner asked a judge to seal his divorce records. On September 5, the *Atlantic Monthly*'s blogger Andrew Sullivan published an item entitled "Here We Go," where he wrote: "Todd Palin's former business partner files an emergency motion to have his divorce papers sealed. Oh God." The clear implication of this item, published on the Web site of what was once the most prestigious literary and intellectual journal in America, was that the only possible reason the business partner would want to have his divorce records sealed would be to protect the Palins from evidence of infidelity.

This wasn't the case at all; the man just wanted to protect his privacy. He wisely understood that the ravenous media would track down every last one of Sarah Palin's associations in a search for damaging information. That the reputation of Palin's associates might be harmed as a result was not the media's concern.

"Is the party of traditional marriage aware," Sullivan wrote in a follow-up blog published that day, "that the vice-presidential nominee actually eloped with her now-husband?" This was the entire substance of Sullivan's post. Here was yet another example of the anti-Palin bloggers' disturbing competition to publish any datum about her in the most hysterical fashion possible. To answer Sullivan's question: Is the party of Palin hatred aware that an elopement is a marriage? Why should the "party of traditional marriage" be bothered by a politician who has been married to the same man for more than twenty years?

One of the most popular liberal blogs, Joshua Micah Marshall's Talking Points Memo, hosted a blog entry by one "MarkB," who wrote on September 5 that "there are indications of possibly two affairs. 1. My sources in Alaska say the incident occurred in mid-1990s, right around the time she became mayor of Wasilla. Todd Palin's partner in a Polaris snow machine dealership in Wasilla, Brad Hanson, and Sarah were reportedly flirtatious but never consummated the relationship. When Todd found out, he reportedly dissolved the partnership and sold the dealership. Hampton [*sic*] is now a member of the Palmer City Council. He was married at the time of the reported flirtation."

This was rumormongering character assassination pretending to be "reporting." The blogger could not even keep Brad Hanson's name straight. But, from the vantage point of anonymity, MarkB could sully Palin's character with impunity. And his liberal readers, already inclined to believe the worst about Palin, lapped it up. No one could stop the hate.

On August 30, another anonymous blogger, "ArcXIX," wrote on the left-wing Daily Kos Web site: "Well, Sarah, I'm calling you a liar. And not even a good one. Trig Paxson Van Palin is not your son. He is your grandson. The sooner you come forward with this revelation to the public, the better." ArcXIX posted video purportedly taken in

February 2008, when "Sarah is seen trim, and walking around all of Juneau, Alaska." Those who appended comments to liberal blogs like Daily Kos used the foulest rhetoric, heaping insult after insult in often profane language.

ArcXIX believed that Trig was actually Bristol Palin's son, and that Sarah Palin had passed him off as her own in order to protect her daughter's reputation. As fantastical as it may seem, the idea was widespread throughout the Palin-hating community. The day after ArcXIX made the allegation, Internet impresario Matt Drudge linked to a story about the post on his highly trafficked Web site, magnifying its effect. A reporter for ABC News contacted the McCain campaign, asking for information on the maternity rumors. A McCain staffer called Drudge and asked him to remove the link to the scurrilous item. Drudge complied but the story did not go away.

Sullivan's blog was a clearinghouse for every ad hominem attack on the governor one could imagine. On August 31, he wrote a blog post with the title "Things That Make You Go Hmmm" that linked to ArcXIX's post. The "rumors buzzing across the Internet and the press corps are unfounded and unseemly," Sullivan wrote. ". . . But the noise around this story is now deafening, and the weirdness of the chronology sufficient to rise to the level of good faith questions." Sullivan called on the McCain campaign to "provide medical records for Sarah Palin's pregnancy." The blogs followed furiously from there. In a 7:13 p.m. post that day, Sullivan claimed that "this baby"—i.e., Trig—"was a centerpiece of the public case for Palin made by the Republicans. They made it an issue—and therefore it is legitimate to ask questions about it." No they didn't, and no it wasn't.

Also on August 31, in a headline for an article about Trig on his eponymous Web site, Michael Moore wrote: "Show Us the DNA!" The text was later removed.

Sullivan provided his readers with links to the list of births at the Mat-Su hospital on the day Trig Palin was born, as well as photos of Palin during her pregnancy so that his audience could determine whether she had ever been with child. It was do-it-yourself investigative journalism. Try to spot the baby bump on Palin's belly. In 2005, when then-Senate majority leader Bill Frist diagnosed Terri Schiavo's mental state from a videotape, liberals howled in protest. Now they were doing much the same thing, attempting to divine the maternity of a child by scouring pixilated images and constructing elaborate chronologies of Palin's pregnancy from conception to delivery. And since reporters read left-wing Web sites with regularity, they began to bring up Trig in conversations with McCain advisers.

The whole thing was too much. Left-wing bloggers were feeding the beast fantastic stories about Sarah Palin, and the press—convinced that Palin had not been "properly vetted" because they had never heard of her—ate up every last piece of dirt. Knowing that the frenzy was spinning out of control, the McCain campaign announced on September 2 that seventeen-year-old Bristol was five months pregnant. This proved definitively that Trig was not Bristol's child. Do the math. Bristol had been carrying her baby since March. Trig was born in April. It was thus physically and chronologically impossible for Bristol to be Trig's mother. A rational man—who wouldn't have doubted that Sarah Palin was Trig's mother to begin with, because *why on earth would she lie about something like that*—would have heard the news about Bristol and said, *Well, that settles it.*

But the Palin-haters are not rational. Hatred is an emotion. It has nothing to do with the intellect. Even after the McCain campaign disclosed Bristol's pregnancy, Sullivan kept e-mailing communications personnel requests for comment on Trig's genealogy. On September 2,

Sullivan wrote Goldfarb: "Can you answer this question for me: Were Governor Palin's medical records part of the vetting process?"

Goldfarb did not respond.

Sullivan could not let the matter go. On September 16, he wrote to both Goldfarb and RNC tech guru Liz Mair: "I'm very sorry to say, it's come to this: Can you confirm on the record that Trig Palin is Sarah Palin's biological son? Or could you tell me who is the person on the McCain campaign who can give me a factual on-the-record confirmation? We still don't have it. I've now read and re-read and re-read the three stories in the public domain in the [*Anchorage Daily News*] and [*New York Times*] and the two stories in the *National Enquirer* and there is as yet no objective evidence that it is. Since this is a crazy idea, it should be easy for you or someone to let me know, the most popular one-man political blog site in the world, what the truth is. I will publish that statement with no adornment just as I published the statement Michael sent to me a while back. All I am interested in is the truth. Please let me know ASAP. I need a response from you guys for a story on deadline. Again the question is: 'Can you confirm on the record that Trig Palin is Sarah Palin's biological son?'"

The campaign did not dignify this query with a response. A day later, however, Sullivan wrote again: "It's now been twenty-four hours since I asked an obvious factual question. My blog has the biggest readership of any one-person political blog on the planet. I asked a simple question akin to asking whether you can confirm that the sky is blue. Here's the question in case it got lost."

Sullivan repeated his question.

Then he went on: "Can I please get a response of some sort, even if it is that you will not respond? That in itself is worth reporting. If I do not get an answer to my question by tomorrow morning, I will post the time and date I asked the question and let my readers know you refuse to respond. And let them make a judgment as to why. What else can I do?"

Then, more than a month after Bristol Palin's pregnancy was a matter of public record, Sullivan wrote Mair and Goldfarb once more: "I'd appreciate it if this email were not forwarded to other reporters. There is a public record of babies born at Mat-Su Regional Medical Center for April 2008. Here's the list."

Sullivan provided a link.

He continued: "[T]he hospital confirmed on the phone that, as a general rule, they ask all parents if they are happy to have their baby listed there. May I ask if the Palins were asked by the hospital? And if they were asked, why did they choose not to include Trig Palin in the list of other Wasilla babies at the hospital? As always a prompt reply is appreciated. I'd like to include the reply in a forthcoming post to ensure that your point of view and the fairest summary of the facts is conveyed to my readers."

"I'm not that convinced that that's her baby," comedian Bill Maher said of Trig on his cable talk show *Real Time* on September 5, 2008. Clearly, Sullivan shared Maher's opinion. Sullivan's e-mails to the McCain campaign were attempts to invade Palin's privacy in a manner the blogger would never, ever, sanction if Barack Obama were involved. Reading the correspondence, you are struck by Sullivan's earnestness. The desperation with which he continued to ask for information about Trig's maternity is almost pitiable. His continuing obsession with Trig and his mother, Sarah, is almost too much to bear.

The larger mystery is what the conspiracy theorists thought was actually going on. Let's say, for the sake of argument, that the goons are right. If Trig is neither Sarah's nor Bristol's child, then, whose child is he? Taking the conspiracy theorists' logic to its absurd conclusion means accepting that Sarah Palin—the governor of America's largest state—decided, for no apparent reason, to kidnap someone's Down syndrome infant and raise him as her own. It means accepting that Palin wanted to fool everybody, to conjure up an imaginary backstory, with no regard for the possible consequences. It means denying that Palin is a regular human being, a mother, a talented politician whose reputation rests on straight talk. It means, instead, believing that Palin is a liar of pathological magnitude. An incredibly talented con artist. An evildoer.

The conspiracy theorist develops complex explanations for phenomena he finds difficult to accept or understand. He is convinced that powerful figures work behind the scenes to control the destiny of ordinary men. The left-wing conspiracy theorist shares these beliefs but applies them only to conservatives and Republicans. For him, conservatives are always out to lie, cheat, steal, kill, and profit at someone else's expense. He does not see conservatives as human. He sees them as demonic. He cannot fathom that Republicans might be regular people with large and happy families. He cannot accept that those families might have problems just like everybody else's. There is always another, more lurid explanation. *There are indications of possibly two affairs. I'm not that convinced that that's her baby.* Such drivel says a lot more about those who spout it than about Sarah Palin.

Amazingly, a few mainstream media outlets parroted the conspiracy theorists' claims. The September 2, 2008, *Los Angeles Times* reported that the McCain campaign had disclosed Bristol Palin's pregnancy "to rebut Internet rumors that the governor's four-month-old baby, Trig, is in fact Bristol's child." On the same day, the *New York Times* breathlessly conveyed that "the Palins' statement arrived after a flurry of rumors had made their way through the Internet over the weekend, growing and blooming, it seemed, by the minute. Some claimed that Ms. Palin had not actually given birth to Trig, but that Bristol had, and that the family had covered it up. Various Web sites posted photographs of Ms. Palin in the months leading up to his birth this year, and debated whether her physique might have been too trim for her stage of pregnancy." On September 7, 2008, the *Washington Post* reported that "Palin's account" of her pregnancy "inspired astonishment, as well as an Internet rumor—that the governor had rushed home not to deliver her own child, but to pretend to deliver her daughter's—that was so powerful the McCain campaign said it was announcing Bristol's condition to knock it down."

The astute reader will note that the *Post* reporting team, which included a Pulitzer Prize winner, described the fantastic lies as "powerful" and did not explicitly rebut them. Even months after the election, in an April 18, 2009, article on Palin's speech to a pro-life group in Evansville, Indiana, the *Washington Post* attributed the smear to Palin's "reticence" about "her son's condition or the circumstances surrounding his birth."

Most of the media did not fall into the fever-swamps, however. They were content to take simpler, less crackpot jabs at Palin's youngest son and her performance as a mother. On August 30, liberal commentator Alan Colmes asked, in a blog post on Alan.com, "Did Palin Take Proper Pre-Natal Care?" Did Alan Colmes's mother teach him any manners? On September 10, in the *Nation,* columnist Katha Pollitt wrote that Trig was a "campaign prop." It was a further example of the liberal tendency to refer to this newborn child as an inanimate object.

The mainstream media's primary interest was in whether Palin could hold high office and still raise a family. "Children with Down's syndrome require an awful lot of attention," CNN's John Roberts said on August 29. "The role of vice president, it seems to me, would take up an awful lot of her time, and it raises the issue of how much time will she have to dedicate to her newborn child?" ABC's Bill Weir asked campaign strategist Mike DuHaime, "The Palin family also has an infant with special needs. What leads you, the senator, and the governor to believe that one won't affect the other in the next couple of months?" NBC reporter Amy Robach introduced a September 3 *Today* segment by asking, "The broader question, if Sarah Palin becomes vice president, will she be shortchanging her kids or will she be shortchanging the country?" At a D.C. luncheon I attended in October 2008, a famous Beltway journalist wondered aloud—this is not a joke—why Palin was running for office when *every* Christian conservative thinks mothers should work only in the home.

To some degree, these questions (except the last one) were valid. Raising five kids is not easy, especially when one of the children has Down syndrome. But the Palins have shown that they are up to the task. After all, Palin was able to raise four children while running a successful gubernatorial administration. And between Trig's birth and the time she resigned from office in July 2009, Palin did the same job with five kids. The Palin family has a part-time stay-at-home parent in Todd, when he's not on his snow machine or fishing or on the North Slope or pursuing small business opportunities. The kids are fully integrated into the governor's professional life.

Palin didn't even take off from work the day she delivered Piper. She treated labor like a routine visit to the doctor's office. She juggles motherly duties with political responsibilities. Her style of motherhood may not live up to many people's expectations, but it seems to have worked well enough for her, her husband, and her children. Aren't they the ones who matter most?

Not to the press, whose narcissism knows no bounds. Their jurisdiction is global. They are the court of first resort and final appeal. And their sentence *in re* Sarah Palin was nothing less than cruel and unusual.

THE MODERN PHARISEES

The revelation that her eldest daughter was pregnant added force to the Palin shock wave. The day the news was announced—September 2, 2008—the *New York Times* published six stories referring to Bristol, including three on the front page (two of which were above the fold). The *Washington Post* also broadcast Bristol Palin's pregnancy from the top of its broadsheet. The editors apparently gave no thought to the effect that it might have on the young woman, her family, and the child she was carrying.

It was hard to say what made the story so important. In a speech the following year, Palin said that Bristol had told her parents she was pregnant in May 2008. The family had tried to keep the information secret, though they didn't do a great job. Most Alaskans, especially those who lived in greater Anchorage, had some idea Bristol was going to have a baby. They greeted the rumors with shrugs. Such is life, they thought. Other things mattered more.

The national press had a different reaction. Almost all its members greeted Sarah and Todd Palin's statement on Bristol with a mixture of shock, condemnation, and perverse delight. "For all the confidence expressed by Republicans here," Adam Nagourney wrote in the September 2, 2008, *New York Times,* "it is too soon to judge whether this is just a blip—the kind of event that will be forgotten in a news cycle or two—or one of those events that help shape the narrative of the campaign." "[I]f it is followed by more disclosures about Ms. Palin," Nagourney wrote, ". . . that is one thing that delegates are worried about as the portrait of this unknown woman plucked from Alaska is filled in in the days and weeks ahead." The unstated hope was that "this unknown woman plucked from Alaska" was carrying with her a load of baggage so heavy, it would collapse the McCain campaign.

For once, you would have thought the press would behave like adults and treat the matter fairly, courteously, and quietly. That did not happen. After the story broke, two prominent reporters on the religion beat phoned Michael Cromartie, the vice president of the Ethics and Public Policy Center in Washington, D.C. *It's over,* the reporters told Cromartie in separate conversations. *What's over?* Cromartie asked. *The election,* came the reply. Bristol Palin's pregnancy would doom Palin with the GOP's Evangelical base. The Christians would revolt at the immorality of an unwed teenager getting pregnant. And with the Republican core refusing to vote for McCain-Palin, Obama-Biden would win in a landslide.

Cromartie disagreed. The media didn't understand what they were dealing with. "They're all sitting around hoping McCain will implode," Cromartie told me, "and here comes this news that just might do it. They're looking through this paradigm that says Evangelicals want to condemn, and it's simply not true. The modern megachurches are full of people who come to the faith maybe later in life, they've raised children, they've faced the same problems everyone does encountering the culture. But Evangelicals today talk more about forgiveness than judgment."

James Dobson, for instance. He is one of the country's most famous social conservatives. He released a gracious, charitable statement on Bristol that lauded her decision to keep the child and marry the father. Other leaders in Evangelical circles said similar things. Indeed, the Bristol experience proved that the caricature of Bible-toters ready to tear down the wall separating church and state, of Christians chomping at the bit to start an American Taliban, is bunk. People are more complicated than that. They make mistakes. They slip up. They sin. They look for forgiveness and grace. That is one way many of them find God. Lucky for Bristol, she had a family and a church that accepted her, and stood ready to assist her.

The media, however, wanted to chastise her. They are the new Pharisees: legalistic, moralistic, condemnatory of those they deem ethically inferior. Media critic Michael Wolff captured the liberal attitude in a post on his Off the Grid blog on March 12, 2009: "Bristol and Levi and their story of teenage sex and family dysfunction defined Sarah Palin," he wrote, "making her as large a star as any failed vice-presidential candidate has ever been, and helped doom the McCain campaign. Palin obviously slipped her daughter's pregnancy past the McCain people, who, looking foolish and incompetent for being unaware, then had to embrace the whole mess as grand political strategy." Such inaccurate and unconvincing analysis—Palin told McCain about Bristol before he chose her, and there are no grounds to say Palin "helped doom" McCain—was par for the course wherever liberal Democrats gathered.

Partisan Democrats went especially overboard where Bristol Palin was involved. They said things they would never say about a child of Democratic parentage. "It's conceivable a seventeen-year-old girl just screwed the GOP," Berkeley academic George Lakoff told *US Weekly* on September 2, 2008. "Don't you want your president to have had the presence of mind to have chatted to her teenage kids for five minutes about birth control?" David Letterman asked during his September 3, 2008, show. The British comedian Russell Brand, before hosting the *MTV Video Music Awards* in September, told the *Daily Telegraph* that the show's producers asked him "to tone down the gags about Sarah Palin. I wanted to say she was forcing her teenage daughter to have a baby because she is so antiabortion. But also, as a Republican, she is pro-execution so she is going to give her the electric chair for being a little slut. They weren't keen on that one."

Imagine that.

Some liberals went so far as to suggest a racial double standard. On the September 3 episode of *The View*, liberal comedienne Joy Behar said, "They're white, they're Christian. Everybody loves them on the right wing. But if this was a black teenage couple . . ." She repeated the line in October, when she asked, "Where is Sarah Palin's family values here? I don't understand that." Then she said, "If this was a black teenager that was pregnant, Obama's kids, God forbid, they would be all over it like a cheap suit and you know it."

In fact, we do not know that "they would be all over it." Quite the opposite. If by "they," Behar meant religious conservatives, she ought to have known that communities of faith do more charitable work in blighted places, help more people regardless of race, than liberal comediennes might care to admit. Behar, like the reporters who called Michael Cromartie, was working from anachronistic premises. In her mind, believers are zealots with foam shooting out of their mouths, vestment-wearing Neanderthals eager to pin scarlet letters on every last single mom in the country. In her mind, "they" are all white and exhibit charity and compassion only toward those who look as they do.

Bristol's pregnancy was an integral component of the liberal attempt to portray Sarah Palin as a pretender. Central to this effort was the incorrect idea that Palin was against contraception. On September 1, 2008, a blogger for the Center for American Progress, Matthew Yglesias, wrote that the "Palin family sticks with anti-abortion, anti-contraception, anti–single motherhood principles and arranges [a] shotgun wedding for Sarah and Todd Palin's 17-year-old daughter." On September 2, 2008, the *Washington Post* columnist Ruth Marcus wrote that "Sarah Palin opposes programs that teach teenagers anything about contraception." In a September 10, 2008, post on The Corner, the conservative radio host Michael Graham wrote that he had received an e-mail from CNN saying Palin "earned her conservative bona fides with an adherence to conservative Christian principles against sex education." On September 16, 2008, Timothy Noah wrote on Slate.com that

Palin "opposed teaching teenagers about contraception," citing Ruth Marcus's column as evidence. And on October 9, 2008, the *Washington Post* published an op-ed by Amy Schalet, an assistant professor of sociology at the University of Massachusetts, Amherst, stating that Palin supported "policies that prohibit teachers from explaining the benefits of contraception and condoms."

This was all bosh. "I'm procontraception," Palin said in an August 2006 radio debate. In 2008, Palin told Katie Couric, "Well, I am all for contraception. And I am all for preventative measures that are legal and safe." The *Washington Post* was forced to issue a correction to Schalet's op-ed. But by that point the big lie—that Palin was anticontraception—had hardened. In the liberal imagination, it had become unfalsifiable.

The press put forward specious arguments to show that Palin was a hypocrite. One was that Palin had cut the education budget for special needs children. The claim was first made on the Daily Kos on September 3, 2008: "Palin cut Special Education budget by sixty-two percent," read the blog's title. The author, "Night Runner," linked to the anti-Palin Alaska blog Mudflats, which published budget documents detailing a decline in appropriations for the Special Education Service Agency (SESA) between 2007 and 2008. "Hilzoy," a blogger for the *Washington Monthly,* published an item on September 4, 2008, which claimed that "Palin actually slashed funding for schools for special needs kids by sixty-two" percent. Matthew Yglesias repeated the claim in a post that day, too. Also on September 4, on CNN, Soledad O'Brien asked Palin spokeswoman Nicolle Wallace, "One [thing] . . . that has certainly gotten people sending me a lot of e-mails is the question about, as governor, what she did with the special needs budget, which I'm sure you're aware, she cut significantly, sixty-two percent I think is the number from when she came into office." O'Brien did not mention that the figure originated in the left-wing blogosphere. Perhaps she did not know where the number came from.

If O'Brien had known the statistic's provenance, she might have been more circumspect. The 62 percent figure was an outright fraud. Palin had not cut the special needs budget. Rather, she increased it— dramatically. One arrived at 62 percent from an incorrect reading of Alaska's budget documents. As "Hilzoy" later acknowledged in a correction, "funding for the Alaska Challenge Youth Academy was broken out into its own budget category, which accounts for the drop in funding for the original item." In truth, according to an article published in the online edition of *Education Week* on April 29, 2008, Palin's budget increased "spending for students with special needs to $73,840 in fiscal 2011, from the current $26,900 per student in fiscal 2008, according to the Alaska Department of Education and Early Development."

Another flawed argument was that Palin had "slashed funding for teen moms," as a headline in the online September 2, 2008, *Washington Post* put it. The *Post* article reported that Palin had used her line-item veto to cut "funding for Covenant House Alaska"—which the post described as "a mix of programs and shelters for troubled youths, including Passage House, which is a transitional home for teenage mothers"—"by more than twenty percent, cutting funds from $5 million to $3.9 million."

Yet the Rhode Island blogger Carroll Andrew Morse (Anchor Rising.com) demolished the *Post*'s claim in a September 3, 2008, post. "Covenant House asked the Alaska legislature to provide $10 million, the legislature answered with $5 million in the 2009 budget," Morse wrote. "Governor Palin cut the figure back to $3.9 million—for this year. This likely doesn't stop the expansion; Covenant House will either have to get more from the state in a future year and/or increase the amount from private donations to make it happen. But no existing program that helps teenage mothers or the children of teenage mothers has been affected by this budget decision, and *calling a one-time infusion of $3.9 million added by the state on top of normal operating expenses a 'cut' only makes sense if you can't do math, if you don't understand the difference between a capital outlay and an operating outlay, or if you hate Republicans*" (emphasis added).

The mistaken idea also spread that as mayor of Wasilla Palin had taken steps to ensure that rape victims paid for the cost of their post-trauma medical exams. But the matter is more complicated than that. The *New York Times* could not find any evidence that Palin had ever voiced an opinion on the matter. And a report on CNN.com concluded that "interviews and a review of records turned up no evidence that Palin knew that rape victims were being charged in her town."

The legislative sponsor of the Alaska bill mandating that municipalities pay for rape kits was Eric Croft, a partisan Democrat who kept up the criticism during the fall 2008 campaign. Croft's main talking point was that he found it inconceivable that Palin had been unaware of the policy his bill forbade. Yet it is entirely conceivable that Palin did not know what was going on. Her leadership style is to set priorities and delegate responsibility. And there was no line item in the Wasilla budget devoted to rape kits that Palin could have cut.

Money for the exams fell under the heading "contractual services." Palin did cut the money allocated there, but "contractual services" included a variety of expenditures, and nothing tied the mayor to the specific policy of charging women for rape-kit examinations. Her only public comments on the issue came in 2008, when she was forcefully opposed to the idea that the victim should "pay for anything." Either Palin is a genius at orchestrating major policy changes behind the scenes and then covering her tracks so that no one can trace her involvement years in the future, or her budget cuts inadvertently left the Wasilla police department in a position where they looked uncaring.

Why did all these pernicious falsehoods hold such power? Why were Democrats and the media frenetically attempting to expose Palin as a hypocrite? In retrospect, the fight over Sarah, Trig, and Bristol Palin looks a lot like a proxy fight over abortion rights. On September 4, on Slate .com, Hanna Rosin wrote: "In the pantheon of family values, avoiding abortion sits at the top, above marriage or staying home to raise your children." On September 6, also on Slate, Jacob Weisberg wrote: "If you do not allow teenage girls who accidentally become pregnant to have abortions, you are demanding either that they raise their children as single mothers or that they marry in shotgun weddings." The Bristol Palin option, Weisberg continued, "doesn't promote family happiness, stability, or traditional structure, either." On September 9, in an On Faith blog post at WashingtonPost.com, Wendy Doniger wrote: "As for sex, the hypocrisy of her outing her pregnant daughter in front of millions of people, hard on the heels of her concealing her own pregnancy (her faith in abstinence applying, apparently, only to non-Palins), is nicely balanced by her hypocrisy in gushing with loving support of her teenage daughter after using a line-item veto to cut funding for a transitional home for teenage mothers in Alaska." Then there was Carol Fowler and her (later retracted) aphorism that Sarah Palin's "primary qualification seems to be that she hasn't had an abortion."

When liberals looked at Sarah Palin, one of the first things they saw was a pro-life mother of five whose teenage daughter was also pregnant. They saw a striking, captivating refutation of the idea that women must trade off child rearing for professional success. They saw a family that did not think an unwanted pregnancy was shameful. They saw a mother and daughter who believed in the rights of the unborn and who were prepared to make personal sacrifices in order to bring unintended pregnancies to term.

All this challenged long-held elite norms. For social liberals, both Democratic and Republican, pregnancy is something to be avoided until the child can be reared in the optimum socioeconomic environment. That is why contraception should be freely available and abortion legal. Whatever rights the unborn may have are subordinated to the autonomy and freedom of the baby's mother. The best expositor of this position is also the most famous. Campaigning in Johnstown, Pennsylvania, on March 29, 2008, Barack Obama said, "Look, I got two daughters—nine years old and six years old. I am going to teach them first about values and morals, but if they make a mistake, I don't want them punished with a baby." For Obama and his compatriots, a new life can be a penalty. The Palins flagrantly defied this liberal tenet, and they took vicious criticism for it.

One might think that the McCain campaign would be terrified to face the press with the news that Bristol Palin was pregnant. That was not the case. To some extent, the campaign was relieved. "The baby was how we cleared the decks and caught our breath," Goldfarb said. "Because we finally had an answer for the media. It was: '[Expletive deleted] you. Leave the daughter alone.'"

THE SECOND TRIAL

As the feral beast hounded Palin—reporting false allegations, seeking out rumor and untruth wherever it could find them—the governor was in seclusion. Palin's August 29 debut in Dayton had been an extraordinary success, but she had a lot of catching up to do. She needed to be briefed on John McCain's positions on a wide variety of issues, as well as on how McCain had arrived at those positions. She needed to introduce herself to and coordinate with her new staff: friends of senior adviser Steve Schmidt who had never met Palin and probably had no idea who she was. Finally, she and McCain campaign speechwriter Matthew Scully needed to write the address she would deliver to the Republican convention on September 3. The demands on Palin's time were harsh and unyielding. She spent hours in her hotel suite in the Twin Cities. Outside, a firestorm of bad publicity was taking place in a supercharged, hostile media environment. And Palin could do hardly anything about it.

Palin's introductory rally in Dayton was her first real test as a national political figure. She passed with flying colors. But her second trial, her speech to the convention, was a different matter. This time the world would be watching. Expectations were rising. Every inaccurate report that stated Palin had abused power, lied, betrayed her associates, engaged in affairs, banned books, associated with fringe causes, covered up pregnancies, or spoke in tongues was another potential nail in her political coffin. Over the course of just a few days, her reputation had been cast into a pit of hearsay and vituperation. The only way she could claw out was to deliver one helluva convention speech.

The day Palin spoke, September 3, began with liberals giddy in anticipation. One of them, a *Washington Post* columnist, was so convinced that Palin would crash and burn, he was practically bouncing up and down. To him, Palin was an unqualified idiot from the boonies with a dysfunctional family and no credible political appeal. Her personal charisma and record of accomplishment in Alaska did not phase him. Another reporter, *Time* magazine political writer Mark Helprin, a fellow guest on a radio show on September 1, told me that there was no way "this woman"—i.e., Palin—was qualified to be vice president. There is your nonpartisan and unbiased press. The knives were out.

Traditionally, the vice presidential nominee's speech is little more than a pit stop on the road to the presidential nominee's address. The

2008 GOP convention in St. Paul broke that tradition. Walking around the convention hall, there was no question that the week's most highly anticipated speaker was Palin. No one knew what to expect. Conservative Republicans instinctively liked Palin, but the media were portraying her in the harshest possible light. Would she live up to the hype? Or would she fail miserably and bring McCain down with her?

Palin's opening act was Rudy Giuliani, who got the audience hopping but also ran far longer than his allotted time. The convention organizers had to scrap the planned biographical video introducing Palin to the global television audience. They went straight to the highly anticipated main event.

"Ladies and gentlemen," the announcer said to a cheering conventional hall, "the governor of Alaska . . ."

The cheers grew deafening.

". . . and the next vice president of the United States . . ."

The moment had arrived.

"SARAH PALIN!"

The applause lasted several minutes. Then Palin was off. The speech was a stem-winder; the audience was hers. "Our family has the same ups and downs as any other," she said at one point, introducing her husband and children to the country. "The same challenges, and the same joys. Sometimes even the greatest joys bring challenge. And children with special needs inspire a very, very special love."

What was most remarkable about Palin's speech was that it came from someone who was attending her first Republican National Convention. She did not come across as a neophyte, however. Not one bit. She performed like a veteran. She did not miss a beat when the TelePrompTer briefly malfunctioned. She knew exactly which lines to emphasize, which lines would draw the most applause. She was at ease at the podium enough to make her famous quip. "I love those hockey moms," she said. "You know they say the difference between a hockey mom and a pit bull? Lipstick."

She was tough and unapologetic. She had no problem fitting into the established veep nominee role of attack dog. "Before I became governor of the great state of Alaska," she said, "I was mayor of my hometown. And since our opponents in this presidential election seem to look down on that experience, let me explain to them what the job involves. I guess . . . I guess a small town mayor is sort of like a community organizer, except that you have actual responsibilities."

Palin drew a parallel between her battles against established powers in Alaska and her shabby treatment at the hands of established sources of opinion in the national media. "Well, I'm not a member of the permanent political establishment," Palin said. "And I've learned quickly these last few days that if you're not a member in good standing of the Washington elite, then some in the media consider a candidate unqualified for that reason alone."

BOOOOOOO!

"But, here's a little news flash for those reporters and commentators: I'm not going to Washington to seek their good opinion, I'm going to Washington to serve the people of this great country."

ROAR!!!!!

The speech ran about forty minutes. When Palin left the stage, she ushered in a new political moment. The Republicans had begun their convention in dismal spirits. They had canceled the first night when Hurricane Gustav struck the Gulf Coast. Many had been happy when Bush decided to address the convention via satellite. The second night had not been any better. Senator Joe Lieberman is an honorable man, but he is not a captivating speaker. By the time Palin finished on the third night, however, the Xcel Energy Center was vibrating with energy. Cheers shook the building. You got the sense that the audience was ready to nominate Palin for president, not McCain. You got the sense that she would not have refused the honor.

The most compelling evidence that Palin's convention address was one of the most effective political communications ever came from my *Washington Post* friend. He had been giddy at the prospect that Palin would fail. But, as she spoke, I could see his hopes slowly dimming. And by the time she finished, my friend could say only that Palin might be able to give a good speech, but the jury was still out on whether she could be vice president. This was a grudging concession that the supposed bimbo from the backwoods was, in fact, a huge political talent and a major threat to Democratic aims.

Palin's stirring oratory wiped the slate clean. She was now a major figure in her own right. She would still be attacked, but not with the ferocity that marked her first week in the public eye (in fact, many of the attacks leveled against her in the future would come from within the McCain campaign). She had faced her second big test as a candidate and aced it.

The McCain campaign quickly understood what a fantastic job Palin had done. They had spent the last several days trying desperately to cope with the media deluge. Now they were ready to celebrate.

When speechwriter Matthew Scully entered the bar where McCain staffers and other political operatives congregated after the speech, the entire room burst into applause. Sarah and Todd Palin showed up about forty-five minutes later. "All these D.C. professionals swarmed her," Goldfarb said. "They acted like little children. And she was in great spirits. And I would say that that was the high point of the campaign."

The high point did not last long, however. The press soon returned to their old habits. Two days after Palin's speech, shortly after 9 p.m., a *Newsweek* writer e-mailed McCain campaign spokesmen with questions for an article closing the next morning. The inquiries were either out of line or had already been answered.

"Did Governor Palin ever smoke marijuana or use any other recreational drugs?" the writer asked.

"Was Governor Palin pregnant with her first child when she married Todd?"

"What is Governor Palin's relationship to the Alaskan Independence Party. Does she support any of the party's philosophy or aims?"

Those on the McCain team could hardly believe their eyes. It was an inquisition. And it would not end.

Chapter Five
Amazing Disgrace: How the Press Went After Palin's Faith

THE schoolmaster leaned back in his chair and frowned. He crossed his legs. He perched his glasses down on his nose. He looked tired. Disappointed. As though he'd rather be somewhere—anywhere—else.

The schoolmaster was impeccably dressed: navy blazer, gray sweater vest, striped red tie, dark slacks, and expensive black shoes. And why shouldn't he have been? Since graduating from Princeton in 1965, he had risen to the pinnacle of his profession. He had wealth, prominence, status, and power. His opinion mattered. Men and women of distinction returned his calls. He lived and worked in the greatest city in the world. But here he was, thousands of miles away from home in godforsaken Alaska, administering an entrance exam to an unworthy student. It was painful, really. A chore.

"Did you ever travel outside the country prior to your trip to Kuwait and Germany last year?" he asked, his voice gravelly and choked.

"Canada, Mexico," the student said. She was clearly startled, and even a little peeved at the question. "And then, yes, that trip. That was the trip of a lifetime, to visit our troops in Kuwait and stop and visit our injured soldiers in Germany. That was a trip of a lifetime and it changed my life."

The schoolmaster wasn't satisfied with her answer.

"Have you ever met a foreign head of state?" he asked.

The student said she dealt regularly with trade delegations from foreign powers.

That was the wrong response. "I'm talking about somebody who's a head of state," the schoolmaster snapped. "Who can negotiate for that country. Ever met one?"

"I have not," the student said. "And I think if you go back in history, and if you ask that question of many vice presidents, they may have the same answer that I just gave you."

The student was right, of course. Where does the Constitution say that the vice president or president must have met a foreign head of state before taking office? But that did not bother the schoolmaster. His judgment had been set from the start. He was Charles Gibson, anchor of ABC's *World News Tonight,* and the test he had designed for Governor Sarah Palin was nearly impossible to pass. He asked every question in a condescending tone. The correct answers—i.e., liberal policy positions—were entirely subjective. This exacting standard meant that the vice presidential candidate would not meet the criteria for admission. That the student did not defer to her "better" heightened the tension and intensified Gibson's disdain. Palin had the temerity to defend her qualifications, her positions on issues such as gun rights, abortion, and global warming, her decisions on the Bridge to Nowhere and Troopergate. The nerve! Worst of all for Gibson, Palin emerged from the exam relatively unscathed.

Gibson did land half a punch when he asked Palin if she supported the Bush Doctrine. "In what respect, Charlie?" she asked, hoping Gibson would clarify. That was a mistake. Gibson was not there to help. He was there to poke and prod until Palin uttered a gaffe or malapropism that would make headlines and hurt her political future. *Tell me what you think the Bush Doctrine is,* Gibson said. Palin responded that she supported President Bush's efforts to protect America from attack. Gibson huffed. "The Bush doctrine, as I understand it," he said, "is that we have the right of anticipatory self-defense, that we have the right to a preemptive strike against any other country that we think is going to attack us." The veteran broadcaster had his first *gotcha* moment.

One takeaway from the Gibson interview, then, was that Palin had no clue what the Bush Doctrine is. But this was not as bad as some pretended. Hardly anybody knows what the "Bush Doctrine" is. Doctoral candidates in international relations write entire dissertations trying to pin the phrase down. The man who coined the term, the columnist and Palin critic Charles Krauthammer, wrote in the *Washington Post* on September 13, 2008, that "[t]here is no single meaning of the Bush doctrine. In fact, there have been four distinct meanings, each one succeeding another over the eight years of this administration—and the one Charlie Gibson cited is not the one in common usage today. It is utterly different." The public, and more than a few commentators, may not have been entirely happy with Palin's answer. But they also did not think it disqualified her from office.

The Gibson interview was the first time since Palin's nomination that a network television journalist had the opportunity to ask her questions. Palin was the hottest media commodity around, but the McCain campaign was nervous that she would flop and ruin the Arizona senator's candidacy. Thus, they decided to roll the governor out in dollops to carefully selected networks. This was not how Palin had operated in Alaska. There the press was all around her, and she happily (and sometimes not so happily) interacted with them. Now she spoke to the media only at the direction of her handlers and McCain strategist Steve Schmidt.

It was clear at the time that the McCain campaign had decided on the wrong strategy. The fact that Palin gave so few interviews heightened the stakes and impact every time she spoke to reporters. If Palin had given more interviews right off the bat, there is no question that she would have made the occasional mistake, but the press regimen would also have strengthened her confidence. The blizzard of interviews would have lessened the importance of each individual chat. Palin may have survived the Gibson experience. But she wouldn't be so lucky when she met Katie Couric.

The "Bush Doctrine" exchange grabbed the headlines. In retrospect, however, the most important moment between the governor and the anchor involved religion. In June 2008, weeks before becoming the vice presidential nominee, Palin had visited her old church—Wasilla Assembly of God—where she spoke to a group of graduating students. Palin exhorted the crowd to "pray for our military men and women who are striving to do what is right also for this country, that our leaders, our national leaders, are sending them out on a task that is from God."

The event took place without controversy. When Palin became a national figure, however, video of the speech went viral on the Internet. Shortly thereafter, in an attempt to portray Palin as some sort of theocrat, the press maliciously distorted her words. The lead in Gene Johnson's September 4, 2008, Associated Press story says it all: "Alaska Gov. Sarah Palin told ministry students at her former church that the United States sent troops to fight in the Iraq war on a 'task that is from God.'" This was an utter convolution of what Palin had said. She had asked the students to pray that America was doing the right thing in

Iraq. Nothing more. Furthermore, such a prayer presupposes human fallibility, human weakness, and the real possibility that America may not be doing what God wants it to do. After all, no one knows God's thinking. That's why He's God.

Liberals are supposed to appreciate nuance and complexity. They love to tell us that there are no easy answers. Yet they could not grasp the simple distinction between hoping something is true and asserting it to be true. The plain meaning of Palin's words was there for anyone to see. Her prayer was a commonplace evocation of Lincoln. She wasn't saying God was on America's side. As Palin explained later, she was hoping that America was on God's side. "I would never think it is appropriate to describe the actions of the United States military or the strategies of our commanders as a plan from God," Mercer University ethicist David Gushee wrote in the September 4, 2008, *Wall Street Journal.* Neither would Palin.

For those committed to thinking the worst of Palin, context and plain meaning held no value whatsoever. "Sarah Palin, messenger and messiah," hollered Keith Olbermann during his September 8, 2008, *Countdown.* "[I]f you believe that God is directing troop movements in Fallujah," liberal pundit Rachel Maddow said on the show, "I think that Americans, by and large, will react with the 'what the' reaction rather than the 'neat-o' reaction to that." An hour afterward, on her own MSNBC show, Maddow said that Palin was "asserting that the war is part of God's plan." Later still, Maddow said, "We don't know if she believes in the separation of church and state." Does Maddow believe in the separation of fact from fiction?

The controversy reached its maximum exposure during the Gibson interview. "You said recently in your old church: our national leaders are sending U.S. soldiers on a task that is from God," Gibson told Palin. A grim expression saddened his face. He removed his glasses and paused.

Then, in the televised interview, the ABC producers spliced in a clip from Palin's talk at Wasilla Assembly of God. The video included Palin's statement. Anyone who paid attention to Palin's words would have realized that they did not jibe with Gibson's characterization of them. But the editor included the clip anyway—perhaps in a subtle insult to Gibson's intelligence.

The camera cut back to Gibson and Palin.

"Are we fighting a holy war?" Gibson asked.

"I would never presume to know God's will or to speak God's words," Palin said.

Gibson raised an eyebrow. "But you went on to say that there is a plan, and it is God's plan," he said.

Except Palin had not said that. She had simply asked the students to pray that they, the country, and the country's leaders were following God's wishes. "I believe that there is a plan for this world and that plan for this world is for good," Palin explained, "I believe that there is great hope and great potential for every country to be able to live and be protected with inalienable rights that I believe are God-given, Charlie." In secular terms, she was asking the students to hope that everybody was doing the right thing. The media critic Howard Kurtz wrote in the September 12, 2008, *Washington Post* that Gibson was simply "asking the governor about her own words." No, he wasn't. He was distorting her words. Mangling them. Asking loaded and preposterous questions based on the alterations.

This wasn't journalism. It was theater of the absurd.

A Righteous Double Standard

Why did Gibson's question about "God's plan" matter? Because it put Palin's faith at the center of her candidacy. The exchange signified that the scope of legitimate questions regarding Palin was no longer limited to her qualifications or knowledge or family life. The range had expanded. It now included her personal religious beliefs.

Such a development was not new to presidential politics. Candidates' religions have generated criticism and concern in the past. Probably the most famous example from the twentieth century was John F. Kennedy's Catholicism. When Kennedy ran for president, the Protestant elite worried that the Catholic doctrine of papal supremacy might influence presidential policy. Kennedy said it would not—and he won. More recently, in the 2008 presidential campaign, Mitt Romney also had to answer religious inquiries, regarding his Mormonism. What do Mormons believe? Do they wear special underwear? How would Romney's faith affect his presidency?

The questions revealed a widespread suspicion, even fear, of the candidate's beliefs. Nor could Romney rely entirely on his coreligionists to win. There are far fewer Mormons than there are Catholics (or Evangelical Protestants). The reluctance to vote for a Mormon was enough of a worry that Romney delivered a major speech on religion and American democracy in which he explicitly stated that "no authorities of my church, or of any other church for that matter, will ever exert influence on presidential decisions." The speech earned Romney acclaim from opinion makers, but he still failed to capture the GOP presidential nomination, and it would be hard to argue that anti-Mormon sentiment had nothing to do with it.

Before they moved to Wasilla, the Heath family was Catholic. But the closest church to the family's home was the Wasilla Assembly of God, which was Pentecostal. Sally Heath and her children worshipped there, first for convenience, then out of conviction. Wasilla Assembly of God's founding pastor, Paul Riley, was a major figure in the community. His church had several services and a Bible camp. Sarah Heath was baptized at the camp when she was twelve years old. Sarah Palin's religion, which would generate so much controversy in the future, was accidental. Had a Catholic church been closer, the Heaths would have gone there.

"[W]e went to the church nearest our home," Sally Heath told Lorenzo Benet for his 2009 book *Trailblazer*. "We were able to walk to it. It happened to be the Assembly of God, and eventually we asked to be baptized, and we all did it on the same day. We switched denominations as a matter of convenience, and we fit in very nicely there. They had a wonderful youth group and great activities for the children. Church was an important part of our lives—we didn't have all the other activities kids have today, and back then we went to church twice on Sunday and once in the middle of the week."

To some degree, elite anxiety over Sarah Palin's faith was to be expected. The 2008 election took place after the country had spent eight long years debating the faith of George W. Bush. Bush was a proud and forthright Evangelical Christian. He said Jesus was his favorite philosopher and encouraged government cooperation with faith-based organizations. He was pro-life, opposed to embryonic stem-cell research, and called for a constitutional amendment restricting marriage to a man and a woman. His "compassionate conservatism" prompted the president to increase foreign aid and combat malaria and HIV/AIDS in Africa. Bush was comfortable in his own religious skin and in how it shaped his decisions. Such comfort made his opponents distinctly uncomfortable.

Bush's critics said that he was imposing sectarian beliefs onto public policy debates. The loony fringe went so far as to warn against an impending "theocracy" in the United States. On the other side were Bush's supporters, who pointed out that religious views (or a lack thereof) inform everybody's decisions, and that Bush's faith was a mainstream

Evangelicalism practiced by millions of Americans. The back-and-forth lasted for the entirety of Bush's presidency. But because there are hardly any Evangelicals or conservative Catholics in the media who might report sympathetically on traditionalist faiths, the coverage of Bush's religion slanted toward the views of his opponents. Thus, the conventional wisdom held that Bush's modest and relatively commonplace Evangelicalism hardened his ideological "certainty" and endangered the country by making America the vehicle for the president's messianic religious impulses. Seen in this context, with the press treating Bush's faith with hostility and paranoia, it is hardly surprising that reporters and commentators reacted in such a hysterical manner to Palin's religious beliefs, which are even less connected to the dominant secular culture than those of Bush.

The gap between the forms of faith that the establishment is willing to tolerate in public life and the actual practice of believers is huge. Millions of Americans confess to traditional religious views. Their faith is fluid and diverse. In many ways, Sarah Palin's faith journey exemplifies American religious eclecticism. In 2002 she left the Wasilla Assembly of God for Wasilla Bible, an Evangelical church. When she is in the Alaska state capital, she attends the Juneau Christian Center, which is affiliated with the Assemblies of God. Palin does not identify as a Pentecostal, however. She prefers the term "Bible-believing Christian." The *Time* magazine writer Amy Sullivan described this phrase as a "code phrase." For what? A Christian who believes in the Bible?

Though Palin does not identify as a Pentecostal, the tradition informs her religious beliefs. Pentecostalism is one of the fastest-growing variants of Christianity in the world. "At the end of the [twentieth] century, according to demographers David W. Barrett and Todd M. Johnson, nearly 525 million persons considered themselves Pentecostals or charismatics, making them the largest aggregation of Christians on the planet outside the Roman Catholic Church," writes historian Grant Wacker in his 2001 monograph *Heaven Below*. The Pentecostal tradition emphasizes dramatic expressions of connection with the Holy Spirit. In some churches, that might include speaking in tongues. Palin's "common-sense judgment is based on a subjective religion that pays constant attention to the promptings of the spirit," Ethics and Public Policy Center scholar Michael Cromartie told me. "On-the-spot prayer is not uncommon." In other words, Pentecostalism is an approach to Christianity that seems tailor-made to frighten those liberals who are discomfited by public expressions of religiosity.

No wonder, then, that the press asked Palin questions about her religion that they would never ask Joe Biden or Barack Obama: Did Palin believe that wives should submit to their husbands? Did she think the Iraq war and the Alaska Gasline Inducement Act (AGIA) were missions from God? Was the Bible's every word literally true? Was it appropriate to pray in public? Speaking of prayer, what were hers about? Had she ever spoken in tongues?

The interrogation revealed an ignorance and insecurity that was absolutely staggering. "We have a right to ask how a person's faith intersects with the public performance of their duty," Dr. Richard Land, the president of the Southern Baptist Convention's Ethics and Religious Liberty Commission, told me. "But asking them about the particulars of their faith belief is beyond the pale."

The double standard was egregious. Let me know if you can find an instance where the press asked Joe Biden whether he literally believed in transubstantiation or the Virgin Birth. Nor was the media willing to dwell for long on Barack Obama's Trinity United Church of Christ, where the Reverend Jeremiah Wright propounded an exclusionary Black Liberation Theology. The anti-American, anti-Semitic, racist reverend baptized Barack Obama, presided over his marriage to Michelle Obama, and baptized the couple's children. Obama attended Wright's church for two decades. Yet the media trumpeted the lame excuse that, throughout all those years, Obama had somehow never been aware of Wright's most outlandish and scandalous sermons.

In a March 15, 2008, headline, the *Washington Post* described Wright as a "Preacher With a Penchant for Controversy." That is one way of putting it. Here are some of the Reverend Wright's greatest hits, from the *Post* article: "We bombed Hiroshima, we bombed Nagasaki, and we nuked far more than the thousands in New York and the Pentagon, and we never batted an eye . . . America's chickens are coming home to roost" (the Sunday after September 11, 2001); "We are descendants of Africa, not England . . . We have a culture that is African in origin—not European. The Bible we preach from came from a culture that was not English or European" (Wright's *Blow the Trumpet in Zion!*); "The government gives them the drugs, builds bigger prisons, passes a three-strike law and then wants us to sing 'God Bless America.' No, no, no; God damn America!" (a 2003 sermon); "Racism is how this country was founded and how this country is still run" (a 2006 sermon). Such quotes are just a small taste of Wright's bile.

Obama's friendship and apprenticeship to Wright was no secret. The first time Obama ever heard one of his sermons Wright said, "[W]hite folks' greed runs a world in need." Obama titled his second book after another of Wright's speeches. In a February 22, 2007, *Rolling Stone* story, "The Radical Roots of Barack Obama," Ben Wallace-Wells reported that Obama always knew Wright would be an electoral liability. Yet the media refused to report on Wright for more than a year, until leaked videotape of his most controversial sermons hit ABC News on March 13, 2008. Much as they tried, the media could not ignore the radical reverend any longer. Instead they accepted every anti-Wright statement from the Obama campaign at face value. Anybody who dissented from the Obama line—anybody who suggested that the relationship may have been more complex or damning than the candidate was letting on—was anathema. When Hillary Clinton supporter Lanny Davis went on Anderson Cooper's CNN show in March 2008 and repeated some of Wright's horrible statements, his fellow guest, Joe Klein, the *Time* columnist and Obama supporter, silenced him. "You're spreading the poison right now," Klein said, cautioning Davis that "an honorable person" would know better and "stay away from this stuff." Nor could Davis rely on the television moderator for impartial arbitration. Cooper sided with Klein.

How could it be dishonorable to inform people about the Reverend Wright's noxious politics yet also a reporter's solemn duty to poke and prod at Palin's entire religious history? The discrepancy was not explained.

There was another discrepancy, too. During the entire campaign, the media went out of their way to disabuse voters of the fallacious idea that Obama is a Muslim. Reporters noted in print, television, radio, and the Internet that every time they heard a voter say Obama may be Muslim, they politely told that voter that it was not true and that he or she shouldn't spread the falsehood.

Meanwhile, media gatekeepers left the doors wide open for the most ridiculous caricatures of Sarah Palin, Pentecostalism, and Evangelical Christianity. Myths and stereotypes about Sarah Palin's religion scurried through unobstructed. The media did little to combat the false notion that Palin was a religious zealot who believed the end times were at hand and who could hardly wait to mandate her beliefs on everybody else in the country. Unabated, the left drank thirstily from the well of untruths. No one stopped them. The "poison" was potent only when its victim was Barack Obama.

CASTING STONES

Until Palin arrived on the scene, the most prominent American Pente-costal was probably former senator and attorney general John Ashcroft, whose own faith became a target during his confirmation hearings in the winter of 2001.

Ashcroft survived that confrontation but not before Democrats attempted to write him and the Assemblies of God out of polite com-pany. *Did you know Ashcroft anoints himself with cooking oil?* liberals whispered. *Did you know he doesn't dance?* Rather than embrace America's religious diversity and tolerate different opinions, Democratic interest groups sought to portray Ashcroft as sectarian, sanctimonious, unyield-ing, and imperious. Yet it was they who embodied all these attributes.

Almost eight years after the Ashcroft hearings, the press still had not found a language to describe Pentecostals and Evangelicals without sounding like Margaret Mead among the Samoans. An offensive Pat Oliphant cartoon on the *Washington Post* Web site on September 9 mocked Pentecostals as a bunch of warbling loons. "John McCain's running mate has deep roots in Pentecostalism," wrote Associated Press reporters Eric Gorski and Rachel Zoll in a September 4, 2008, dis-patch. Innocent enough. Yet the reporters went on to call Pentecostal-ism "a spirit-filled Christian tradition that is . . . often derided by outsiders and Bible-believers alike." This was not what you would call the most charitable description possible. Nor was it informative.

On September 28, 2008, the *Los Angeles Times* ran a story titled "Palin treads carefully between fundamentalist beliefs and public pol-icy." The next day, the religion writer M. Z. Hemingway pointed out on her GetReligion.org blog that the Associated Press style guide does not sanction the use of the word "fundamentalist," and for good reason. The word "fundamentalist" is a loaded and inaccurate description of

Palin's belief system. Fundamentalism has a specific historical and theological definition that is different from Pentecostalism or Evangelicalism. Palin is not, strictly speaking, a fundamentalist. The word doesn't apply. That is, unless you are the sort of person who writes headlines for the *Los Angeles Times,* and who probably thinks that *any* conservative believer—anybody, in fact, with strong, non-politically-correct convictions—is a fundamentalist. But deploying a pejorative label in the middle of a newspaper headline is political commentary disguised as just-the-facts-ma'am reportage.

Commentators rarely missed an opportunity to mock or deride Palin's religion. The main locus of the chatter was the *Washington Post's* On Faith blog. A better name for it would be "Attacks On the Faithful." The Palin critics there focused on what they assumed to be the governor's Biblical literalism. "I'd love to know precisely how the Good Lord conveyed to her so clearly his intention to destroy the environment (global warming, she thinks, is not the work of human hands, so it must be the work of You Know Who)," Wendy Doniger wrote on September 9, and "the lives of untold thousands of soldiers and innocent bystanders (He is apparently rooting for this, too, she says), and, incidentally, a lot of polar bears and wolves, not to mention all the people who will be shot with the guns that she thinks other people ought to have. An even wider and more sinister will to impose her religious views on other people surfaced in her determination to legislate against abortion even in cases of rape and in her attempts to ban books, including books on evolution, and to fire the librarian who stood against her."

Doniger laid the nonsense on so thick that it is hard to know where to begin disputing her. For instance, Palin has repeatedly said that mankind may play a role in global warming. She just disagrees with the Green lobby and its subsidiaries in the Democratic Party about how best to address the problem. Furthermore, Palin has *never* said that "the

Good Lord" intended "to destroy" the "lives of untold thousands of soldiers and innocent bystanders" in the Iraq war. That is a revolting sentiment no one in her right mind would support. Palin's purported "determination to legislate against abortion" does not actually exist. The idea that Palin attempted to "ban books" is a gross misrepresentation. And the assertion that she attempted to ban "books on evolution" is a tawdry lie.

To its intended audience, however, the tirade's relationship to facts was not what mattered. What mattered was Palin's politics and how they differed from the accepted liberal positions on the touchstone issues of guns, abortion, and climate change. Criticism of Palin's faith was really criticism of Palin's ideology. The liberal theologian Susan Brooks Thistlethwaite wrote on On Faith on September 3, 2008, that Palin "belongs to Assemblies of God, the largest Pentecostal denomination in the world. Members of the Assemblies of God believe that the Bible in its entirety is verbally inspired by God, is the revelation of God to humanity and is 'the infallible, authoritative rule of faith and conduct.' That means, in a literal reading of scripture, that the authority in the Palin family rests with her husband." Maybe so, though one does get the sense that Sarah Palin is not afraid to exercise authority in the home or anywhere else. Brooks Thistlethwaite probably recognized this, which is why she quickly shifted from a spiritual critique of Palin to a politico-cultural one. "I can tell you flat out," she wrote, "I don't want somebody else in the White House who mouths conservative Christian views, takes us into faith-based wars, will cave in to the oil lobbies, and who does not even understand modern science." Noted. For Brooks Thistlethwaite, the religion talk was a gloss on what was otherwise a standard-issue hit on Palin—though the idea that a Vice President Palin "will cave in" to oil lobbies she defeated twice as governor was laughably novel.

Newsweek's religion editor Lisa Miller embodied the press's estrangement and incomprehension. This was not a surprise. The earnest writer has carved out a niche with her inspired yet daft takes on believers. In the past, for instance, Miller has presented—another way of putting it might be, "invented"—the biblical case for same-sex marriage, and written that Pope Benedict XVI needed to "get better handlers," as if the pontiff were a down-on-his-luck politician. In an April 1, 2009, post on On Faith, Miller expressed puzzlement when she heard that Palin, unable to find someone to pray with, had prayed with her daughter in public. "Sarah Palin, God love her, never lets us down," Miller wrote. What bothered Miller was that Palin expressed her faith in open spaces and felt lonely when no one on the campaign was willing to do the same. But the overall theme of the column was that while God may love Sarah Palin, Lisa Miller does not.

"My prayers," Miller went on, "which are mostly a recognition of gratitude and wonder, are mine alone, whether I'm in a crowd or by myself. Nobody to pray with? What does that mean? Isn't prayer a personal connection between you and your god, whoever or whatever that might be? Did she really need a group to help her pray for her success in the debate? She couldn't do that by herself? Should she have been praying for herself? What about praying alone over a sick child or a dying relative? Praying for those who are starving or for those fight[ing] our wars? Was there no one there worthy enough to speak to God with her? Was her daughter a last alternative?"

Miller's attack on Palin's prayer habits was unhinged. But it also exposed two tendencies in liberal commentary on religion: fascination and repulsion. The former is in constant tension with the latter. On the one hand, Miller's seemingly endless litany of rhetorical questions conveyed an almost voyeuristic desire to understand the thinking and feeling of a prayerful person. But her heated language also suggested that she was frightened by the idea that a woman who wants to pray with others in public might aspire to high office. A genuine curiosity about another's religion clashes against the politically correct idea that some forms of worship—i.e., private, quiet ones—are more socially acceptable than others. The result is writing that is confused and panicky about its subject matter.

Press treatment of Palin's religion was "deplorable and snide," Duke Divinity School professor Grant Wacker, author of *Heaven Below,* told me. Wacker is a Republican who voted for Obama, but he was shocked at the way the media covered the Alaska governor. "They made remarkably little effort to understand the texture of her religion," he said. "The press frequently portrayed it as an aberration, as dangerous. They failed to understand that, in context, her faith was routine."

Shock of the New Media

New media helped foster a biased and incomplete impression of Palin's faith. The recorded images and sound clips that appeared on YouTube without any context played to liberals' worst fantasies. Scurrilous hoaxes zipped around the Internet thanks to e-mail chains and blogs. The advanced communications technology that characterizes the modern world allows individuals to access unmediated information at the speed of light, anytime, anywhere. Stripped of context, however, that information—whether it is contained in video, images, or text—plays to the consumer's emotions just as much as, if not more than, his intellect. The video in which Palin told the crowd at Wasilla Assembly of God to pray that our national leaders are sending our soldiers on "a task that is from God" did not gain widespread currency because liberals were interested in the actual content of Palin's speech. Rather, the clip went viral because its misconstrued content appeared to be confirmation of liberal fears about the vice presidential candidate.

Something similar occurred when video appeared showing the African preacher Thomas Muthee praying over Palin and enjoining God to protect her "from every form of witchcraft." For the supernatural to make a cameo appearance in You Decide 2008 was enough to drive some liberals over the edge. Here was confirmation, they thought, that Palin was a wacko. While mainstream writing on Jeremiah Wright's rancid politics treated him as fairly as possible, and took pains to situate him in his appropriate historical and economic background, the "witch doctor" clip became simply another item in the oversize menu of Palin's alleged extremism.

The video played without any context on Muthee, a well-known speaker at Pentecostal churches. Nor was any second thought given to making an *attempt* to identify with the faith traditions on stage at Wasilla Assembly of God, although those traditions have millions of adherents across the world. Instead, liberals frenetically expressed outrage over the idea that someone who may believe in spirits could be the vice president.

And yet the Catholic Church believes in exorcism. When was Joe Biden asked his thoughts on expunging Satan from human beings? When did the press investigate whether Biden literally believed in the content of the baptismal prayer, where the communicant is asked to reject "Satan and all his works"? Or what about the prayer to Saint Michael the Archangel, which implores Saint Michael to "cast into hell, Satan and all the evil spirits, who roam throughout the world seeking the ruin of souls"?

"It was a flagrantly disproportionate and hypocritical application of the standards of postmodernism to Sarah Palin," Professor Wacker said.

The key point to understand about the Pentecostal tradition, Wacker went on, is its "conviction that God acts supernaturally in history today." Reporters, he went on, "can't get their head around this concept." In some sense, it may have been easier for secular writers to handle radical racial politics than African spiritualism. The space that media types inhabit is filled with bizarre ideologies, from the conspiracism of the 9/11 Truthers to the Marxism of the Spartacist League. But there is no place for spirits and sorcery.

Politics, then, is real to the press in a way that angels, demons, and miracles are not. Many people see forces at work in the world that are beyond human comprehension and understanding. But when a reporter sits down to file a story on religion, she must adopt the positivist attitude that anything that cannot be explained empirically does not exist. Hence, her coverage necessarily will imply that anybody who rejects, or builds upon, Enlightenment precepts regarding religion is irrational and on the fringe. The deck is stacked against believers.

The news that Palin's current church, Wasilla Bible, had hosted Jews for Jesus' executive director David Brickner on August 17, 2008, did not help matters. Wasilla Bible had posted the transcript of Brickner's remarks on its Web site, and the rhetoric was sure to disturb those of us who think that Palestinian terrorism against Israelis is something quite different than God's "judgment" against Jews who have not converted to Christianity. Brickner's remarks traveled from Web site to Web site, causing worry among Jewish voters. This committed Democratic constituency was not disposed to like Palin to begin with. She had already been identified as a pro-life, socially conservative Christian. Her position as a strong supporter of Israel was unknown. And the lie that she had supported Patrick Buchanan had gained currency and fostered a bad impression of her in the Jewish community.

Democrats capitalized on the opportunity. For months, when

compared to the voting bloc's support for previous Democratic nominees, Jewish support for Barack Obama had been tepid. The Democrats could now energize this core group by tarring Palin as a sectarian Christian whose agenda clashed with Jewish voters. On September 2, 2008, the partisan JewsVote.org released an attack statement filled with errors and designed to wreak as much damage as possible. "Given her record as a hard-right Christian conservative," it read, "her embrace of Pat Buchanan, her praise of Ron Paul, and her lack of credentials on foreign affairs, it is likely that her selection would raise serious red flags about the McCain/Palin ticket among Jewish swing voters."

The only true part of the release was the assertion that Palin lacked "credentials on foreign affairs" (as did Barack Obama). The rest was balderdash. In Florida on September 24, 2008, the Democratic congressman Alcee Hastings told an audience that "anybody toting guns and stripping moose don't care too much about what they do with Jews and blacks." This was offensive tripe. And yet Democrats say Republicans are the ones who practice the "politics of fear."

"On the one hand they're saying stop the smears, and on the other they're starting their own smears," Michael Goldfarb told me.

In the end, Jewish voters backed Obama overwhelmingly.

Anonymous Internet hoaxers peddled the idea that Palin was a biblical literalist who believed the universe was less than ten thousand years old. A fake quote attributed to Palin began appearing on various Web sites around August 30, 2008. "God made dinosaurs four thousand years ago as ultimately flawed creatures," the bogus quote read. "[L]izards of Satan really, so when they died and became petroleum products we, made in his perfect image, could use them in our pickup trucks, snow machines, and fishing boats." Palin had never said anything that even closely resembled this ridiculous statement. Yet liberals picked up the myth and ran with it anyway. The anti-Palin Alaskan blogger Philip

Munger, writing at ProgressiveAlaska.blogspot.com on September 3, 2008, wrote that in June 1997, he "took Palin aside" after a town event "to ask about her faith." Palin, Munger went on, "declared that she was a young earth creationist, accepting both that the world was about six-thousand-plus years old, and that humans and dinosaurs walked the earth at the same time." No one else has ever confirmed Munger's account—and even he, just three paragraphs later, wrote that Palin later told him (he provided no date for this second "conversation") that she "was no longer 'necessarily' a young earth creationist." The bottom line is that no one has corroborated Munger's stories.

Yet the unsourced ramblings of left-wing bloggers were confirmation enough for mainstream pundits. The *New York Times* columnist Maureen Dowd wrote on September 6, 2008: "I've got a little news flash for you, Annie Oakley. Dinosaurs disappeared a lot longer than four thousand years ago." On September 10, 2008, the *Huffington Post* quoted the actor Matt Damon: "I need to know if she really thinks that dinosaurs were here four thousand years ago." The British "writer, broadcaster, and Poker player" Victoria Coren wrote in the London *Observer* on October 5, 2008: "This is the woman who believes that God made dinosaurs four thousand years ago, a theory now known as Palintology." Senator John Kerry must have been thinking of such bone-headed sentiments when he said that Palin was part of "the flat-earth caucus."

Palin's name was synonymous with creationism and opposition to Charles Darwin's theory of evolution. The headline on *Wired* writer Brandon Keim's August 29 story was "McCain's VP Wants Creationism Taught in School." "She believes in creationism," wrote *Washington Post* staff writers Amy Goldstein and Michael D. Shear on August 30, 2008. The Wasilla Assembly of God, wrote Evan Thomas and Karen Breslau in *Newsweek* on September 8, 2008, "believes God created the world at every step" (did God rest on the seventh step?).

Of course, Palin's personal thoughts on Genesis were completely ancillary to her performance as a public official. Those thoughts would only matter if Palin attempted to legislate them for everybody. Thus, Brandon Keim asserted in his lead paragraph: "Republican vice-presidential candidate Sarah Palin wants creationism taught in science classes." And in a September 1, 2008, blog on the *Huffington Post*, Arianna Huffington wrote that Palin "wants creationism taught in schools."

This was incorrect. The press tarred Palin as an evolution denier and deemed it relevant because of remarks she had made during an Alaska gubernatorial debate in 2006. Back then, the moderator had asked Palin whether creationism should be taught in schools. She mused that perhaps both sides of the story—evolution, which does not require a Creator, and creationism, which does—might be told in the classroom. But the theory of natural selection ought to have priority. "I say this too as a daughter of a science teacher," she said. The next day, in a radio interview, Palin specifically said that creationism "doesn't have to be part of the curriculum." And according to the *Anchorage Daily News*, Palin clarified that she "would not push the state board of education to add creation-based alternatives to the state's required curriculum." Still later, to Katie Couric, Palin said "science should be taught in science class," and local school boards should design their own curriculums.

How did these common-sense, reasonable sentences—the meaning of which is plain enough—turn into advocacy for creationism "in science classes"? Who knows? For so many in the media, the factual content did not matter. Palin's ideas and expressions had to be twisted and contorted so that she fit the stereotype of the boorish, Luddite religious conservative. If Palin had been allowed to be anything else, it would have complicated the media narrative—and potentially thwarted Barack Obama's glide to the presidency.

THE RELIGIOUS TEST

Sarah Palin is secure enough in her faith that her social policies are flexible and pragmatic. She is a vocal supporter of traditional values, but she also constantly stresses that her "personal opinion" may differ from her administration's actions. As mayor and governor, she did not impose her beliefs on others. She did nothing to introduce creationism into Alaska school curriculums. She governed in a manner consistent with the American mainstream. As the CNN.com writer Randi Kaye admitted on September 8, 2008: "Palin has done little while in office to advance a social conservative agenda." Does anyone doubt that Kaye's story would have been different if the writer had found even *one* piece of evidence that Governor Palin pushed social conservatism on an unwilling populace?

Consider Palin's stance on homosexuality. Like Barack Obama, she opposes same-sex marriage, but that is a fairly common position for a national politician. Otherwise, Palin's record is not easily classifiable. As governor, Palin vetoed a bill denying benefits to the same-sex partners of public employees. During the vice presidential debate, she took great pains to elide any distinction between her position on gay marriage and Joe Biden's—and Biden did not dispute her. What's more, Palin told Katie Couric, "I have, one of my absolute best friends for the last thirty years who happens to be gay. And I love her dearly. And she is not my 'gay friend.' She is one of my best friends who happens to have made a choice that isn't a choice that I have made. But I am not gonna judge people. And I love America where we are more tolerant than other countries are. And are more accepting of some of these choices that sometimes people want to believe reflects solely on an individual's values or not. Homosexuality, I am not gonna judge people."

Not quite Torquemada, is she?

Another example of Palin's pragmatism is her approach to the issue of abortion. In 2007 Palin refused to hold a special session of the legislature on antiabortion legislation. She wanted to hold the special session on AGIA instead—about as far away from a hot-button social issue as you can get. Then, in March 2009, Palin appointed Judge Morgan Christen to the state supreme court. Christen had been a Planned Parenthood board member. The pro-life Alaska Family Council wanted Palin to reject the nomination and take a stand on abortion. Palin did not. She bucked the Alaska Family Council, appointed Christen, and explained on her Sarah PAC Web site why she had made the decision (the other option, she said, would have been worse).

Recently Palin has become more outspoken on the right to life. One of her two major visits to the Lower 48 during her last seven months in office was to a pro-life dinner in Evansville, Indiana. And she expressed support for an Alaska ballot initiative requiring parental notification for teenagers seeking to terminate a pregnancy.

In her support for restrictions on abortion, Palin is squarely in the center of public opinion. The public wants to see fewer abortions, and parental notification and other restrictions, such as a ban on partial-birth abortion, have had no trouble getting passed. Palin is anti-*Roe,* but since the Supreme Court holds ultimate say over American abortion law, there is relatively little a pro-life politician can do to further her cause. Rhetoric, not policy, has been the main outlet for Palin's views.

"I am pro-life," Palin told Charlie Gibson on September 12, 2008. "I do respect other people's opinion on this also. And I think that a culture of life is best for America. . . . Because I know that we can all agree on the need for, and the desire for, fewer abortions in America and greater support for adoption, for other alternatives that women can and should be empowered to embrace to allow that culture of life. That's my personal opinion."

The media attempted to prove that Palin was intolerant. As usual, they got the story wrong. In the November 17, 2008, *Newsweek,* the magazine's writers reported that "the day of the third debate, Palin refused to go onstage with New Hampshire GOP Senator John Sununu and Jeb Bradley, a New Hampshire congressman running for the Senate, because they were pro-choice and because Bradley opposed drilling in Alaska."

This was ludicrous for several reasons. First, Sununu had a 100 percent rating from the National Right to Life Committee. Second, Jeb Bradley wasn't a candidate for the U.S. Senate in 2008. He was a candidate for the New Hampshire senate. Third, Palin appeared at events with many pro-choice figures, including Rudy Giuliani and the former Hillary Clinton supporter Lynn Forester de Rothschild. Fourth, why would Palin refuse to appear on stage with Bradley because he is against drilling in the Arctic National Wildlife Refuge but still pledge to serve as the antidrilling-in-ANWR John McCain's vice presidential candidate? The *Newsweek* story piled illogic on top of illogic.

The governor has repeatedly demonstrated her ability to separate personal opinion from public practice. Palin lives out her values, but she does not seem terribly eager to legislate them. As a gubernatorial and vice presidential candidate, she rarely mentioned social issues on the stump. A promise to promote a "culture of life" is something far different than a commitment to appoint judges who will overturn *Roe v. Wade,* let alone a zeal to pass an absolute ban on abortion. Palin may support the Federal Marriage Amendment, but so do most politicians in the Republican Party and more than a few Democrats. Nor is opposition to abortion and same-sex marriage as far from the mainstream as some in the media would like you to believe. They may not be welcome opinions in sophisticated liberal circles, but they *are* opinions, and elites considered them relatively reasonable and uncontroversial only a few decades ago (in the case of abortion) or less than a decade ago (in the case of gay marriage).

A fair-minded observer would reject the conclusion that Sarah Palin is a religious fanatic, unless "fanatic" is defined down to "someone who believes in God and is not afraid to say it in public." Palin, the "Bible-believing Christian," is not any different from—and in some ways is more moderate than—the countless social conservative politicians who have won office since the Moral Majority came into being in 1979. Palin never banned a single book. She never promoted creationism in public schools. Her antiabortion record is minimalist. The signature issues of her governorship were a natural gas pipeline and an ethics reform bill.

Liberal suspicion of Palin's faith is less about her than it is about the movement and program she is taken to represent. For liberals, unapologetically religious social conservatives threaten the gains that secularism and social liberalism have made in American society since the 1960s. Many of those gains—increased individual sexual autonomy, equality for gay people, tolerance for nonbelievers—were hard fought. The activists who pushed for them do not want to see them disappear. "[L]ike the worst and most terrifying of religious extremists," Cintra Wilson wrote on Salon.com on September 10, 2008, Palin "seems very comfortable with the idea of imposing her own views on everyone else." Yet this is exactly what liberals do when they strive to separate church and state, ban public expressions of Christianity, and secure the right to abortion on demand. Wilson does not have a problem with imposing one's views on others as long as her views are the ones being imposed. Wilson's problem is with imposing *traditional* views on others.

The religious test that liberals apply to politicians in contemporary America is more political than theological. Politicians like Jimmy Carter (before he left the Southern Baptist Convention) and Bill Clinton, who belong to conservative denominations but are functional social liberals, have no problem professing their faith in public. "Bill Clinton mentioned Jesus more in one year than Bush did in eight," Dr. Land said. "But it was okay, because Clinton was using Jesus' name in a politically correct way. You use it to say that we have to help poor people, let the government be Jesus. And your only absolute must be that there are no absolutes. When you believe that, you can invoke Jesus all you want, as the liberal's friend."

Dissent from this creed, however, and no matter your record, there will be a rush to declare you an "extremist" unfit for public office. You'll be the liberal's friend no more. You'll be his enemy.

CHAPTER SIX
Sex and Sarah Palin: The Furious Battle over the Governor's Gender

IT was September 9, 2008, and Barack Obama was making a routine campaign stop in Lebanon, Virginia. During his remarks, Obama spent a few moments telling his audience what the word "change" meant to him. John McCain talks a lot about how he wants change, Obama said, but the Arizona senator was just another rehash of George W. Bush conservatism.

"That's not change," Obama continued. "That's just calling the same thing something different. You know, you can put lipstick on a pig"—this is when the crowd started to crack up—"but it's still a pig. You know, you can wrap an old fish in a piece of paper called change, it's still going to stink after eight years. We've had enough of the same old thing."

Obama may or may not have been referring to Palin's famous line from her convention speech: "You know, they say the difference between a hockey mom and a pit bull? Lipstick." But clearly that's what the crowd thought he was doing. The McCain campaign thought so, too, and immediately went into maximum-outrage mode. The former Republican governor of Massachusetts, Jane Swift, spoke to reporters on a conference call that evening, decrying Obama's remarks as an attack on women in general and women with children in particular. Other surrogates for the McCain-Palin ticket vented as well. The Alaska governor already was being held to a higher standard because she was a woman, McCain aides argued. Now Obama felt free to call her names under the guise of corny aphorisms. The McCain campaign had hoped that Palin's candidacy would spur women voters to abandon Obama, and here was an opportunity to give them a reason to view the Democratic presidential nominee as insensitive. The centerpiece of the McCain counterattack was a twenty-seven-second Web ad juxtaposing Palin's and Obama's jokes, then showing a picture of Obama and stating: "Ready to Lead? No. Ready to Smear? Yes."

The McCain campaign was playing a rather cynical game. Its objective was to embed two ideas in the public mind. The first was that Sarah Palin was an unapologetic postfeminist who did not think her sex was a hindrance and had, in fact, transcended gender politics. The second was that Palin was the victim of the double standard that the media and the opposition party apply to female politicians. One idea clashed with the other. If Palin really didn't care about gender, then why should the double standard bother her? The problem was never solved.

In the early days after Palin's debut, when Palin hatred was burning brightest, the McCain campaign played the victim card more often than it should have done. The glee with which the campaign jumped on the "lipstick on a pig" sound bite was another illustration of its obsession with "winning" the daily news cycle. Steve Schmidt, the driving force behind the campaign, had a background in communications that shaped his priorities. Rather than focus on long-term goals, Schmidt remained preoccupied with daily combat in the media. "Schmidt's a press secretary," consultant Mike Murphy told me. "That's why the whole McCain campaign was about press secretary stuff."

On occasion, Schmidt's desire to shape the news cycle above all else had positive results. The "Celebrity" ad, released in the middle of the summer of 2008 after Obama's trip to Europe, was a brilliant takedown of the Democratic candidate's pretensions. (The ad portrayed Obama as "the biggest celebrity in the world" whose talents and abilities were only skin deep.) Mostly, though, Schmidt's strategy produced little gain. In June, McCain's attempt to step on Obama's victory in the Democratic presidential primary, by delivering a speech of his own moments before Obama's, came across as peevish and uncharitable (the optics of that event—McCain delivering a speech against a lime green background, an old white dude surrounded by other old white dudes—did not help). The "lipstick on a pig" counterpunch seemed more like a trivial distraction than a substantive matter for debate. Later, McCain's surprise announcement that he would "suspend his campaign" to bolster congressional support for the bank bailout, and his request that the first presidential debate be delayed until his work in the Senate was complete, may have shut the door on his presidential ambitions.

The "lipstick on a pig" controversy may have hurt Palin. Her campaign's response bought in to the grievance-mongering one associates with old-school feminism. The political consultant and author Jeffrey Bell, who classifies this school of thought as "adversarial feminism," wrote in the September 15, 2008, *Weekly Standard* that its central tenet is "children and childbearing [are] the central instrumentality of men's subjugation of women." For the adversarial feminists, women are constant victims of misogyny, whether it is conscious or unconscious, apparent or "structural" (and hence invisible to everyone except political activists). The ideology of adversarial feminism is one big gripe. It discounts all the advances women have made over the last century. It conveniently ignores the power that women wield throughout American society and culture.

Palin is aware of this power, and of her unique place on the spectrum of gender politics. In her August 29, 2008, speech in Dayton, Ohio, she paid tribute to Hillary Clinton and portrayed her own candidacy as an extension of the then–New York senator's presidential effort. Palin frequently referred to the "glass ceiling," borrowing a term from the feminist lexicon to describe a lack of advancement due to social injustice. In October 2008, she devoted an entire policy speech to women's issues. Palin understands that she is a role model for young women across the country. As the second woman in American history to have a place on a presidential ticket, Palin is a female trailblazer. And as a prominent and powerful woman, Palin has been subjected to the same tough treatment that women in similar positions have faced throughout history.

In her 1995 book *Beyond the Double Bind: Women and Leadership,* the University of Pennsylvania professor Kathleen Hall Jamieson identified five "double binds," or no-win situations, that "[h]istorically, women have faced and transcended." Among them is "femininity/competence." This is the idea that a woman can be either beautiful and feminine *or* smart and effective, but she cannot be both beautiful *and* smart, feminine *and* effective. No question, Palin is trapped in a similar problem. Her good looks and fecundity cut against her reputation for political savvy and common-sense smarts. American society has no place for a former beauty queen who is also intelligent and conservative, so Palin's enemies went out of their way to portray her as a dumb bimbo. "It's not talked about," Palin 2008 speechwriter Lindsay Hayes said, "because the people who usually talk about it are academics and liberal Democrats, very few of whom supported her candidacy."

And yet Palin's candidacy put adversarial feminists in a double bind of their own. Her à la carte approach to feminism, which adopted the language of empowerment but combined it with pro-life activism, left them stupefied. Support for Palin on the basis of her womanhood might have lent credibility to her politics, which the feminists abhor. Yet opposition to her on the basis of those politics might damage the feminists' claim to speak for their entire sex. Palin's enemies attempted to escape the bind by denying that she was a woman to begin with. "No," Heather Mallick wrote on the Web site of the Canadian Broadcasting Corporation on September 5, 2008, "she isn't even female really. She's a type, and she comes in male form too." Wendy Doniger, in her On Faith blog, wrote on September 9, 2008, "Her greatest hypocrisy is in her pretense that she is a woman." The author Cintra Wilson, writing on Salon.com on September 10, 2008, pronounced, "She ain't no woman." On September 11, 2008, someone claiming to be associated with NOW told Politico, "She's more a conservative man than she is a woman on women's issues" (NOW President Kim Gandy later disavowed the comment). The feminists had graduated from gynecology to ontology. In their universe, chromosomes and anatomy do not confer womanhood. Sympathy with the left wing of the Democratic Party does.

The feminist attempt to expel Palin from the community of women was not unique. It brought to mind black activists' efforts to portray African American conservatives such as Clarence Thomas and Condoleezza Rice as "Uncle Toms" who "aren't really black." By such logic, membership in a group becomes conditional on a subject's willingness to embrace liberal pieties. Politics trumps biology. The left uses this clever rhetorical gambit often. Why is it clever? Because when you deny your opponent's membership in the besieged group, you also deny her status as a victim. And once she is no longer a victim, she can be insulted, disgraced, and lied about with impunity.

"The thought of such an opportunistic anti-female in the White House—in the Cheney chair, no less—is akin to ideological brain rape," Cintra Wilson wrote in her Internet screed. For Wilson, the election of John McCain and Sarah Palin would plunge the nation into a time warp in which women would revert to the social roles they inhabited in some long ago dark age. "I did not think that women being downgraded to second-class . . . chattel would be a pressing concern in my lifetime," Wilson continued. "I thought it was like polio, or witch burning—an inhumane error that had already been corrected. But after eight years of Republican hegemony, and now the potential ascendance of this sheep in ewe's clothing, I am so mortally offended I feel like it is really time for women to be angry, hardcore, and disgusted again." Apparently Wilson's friends felt the same way. "Sarah Palin and her virtual burqa have me and my friends retching into our handbags," she wrote. "She's such a power-mad, backwater beauty-pageant casualty, it's easy to write her off and make fun of her. But in reality I feel as horrified as a ghetto Jew watching the rise of National Socialism."

It was Cintra Wilson's hysteria that was truly sickening. At the same time, though, her fit also disclosed the profound feminist aversion to Palin's nomination. One might think that the folks concerned with promoting women's influence in society would be happy at the prospect of a female vice presidential candidate. But that would be naïve and woolly-headed. On MSNBC on August 29, 2008, Democratic strategist Keith Boykin said Palin's nomination was "an insult to women." Following up on the "insult" theme, Susan Reimer wrote in the September 1, 2008, *Baltimore Sun*: "Does McCain think we will be so grateful for a skirt on the ticket that we won't notice that she's anti-abortion, a member of the NRA, and thinks creationism should be taught alongside evolution?" Then, in a September 28, 2008, interview with *New York* magazine, feminist icon Gloria Steinem also said that Palin's nomination was "such an insult." To whom? To Steinem, presumably. "As social-justice movements have learned the hard way," Steinem said in the interview, "having someone who looks like you and behaves like them—who looks like a friend but behaves like an adversary—is worse than having no one." To which "adversary" was Steinem referring? Men? Conservatives? The tens of millions of American women who disagree with, or have never heard of, Gloria Steinem? The answer is unclear. What is abundantly clear, however, is that Palin was estranged from the adversarial feminists because she had the courage not to subscribe to their party line.

THE FRONTIER FEMINIST

"Palin represented an explosion of a brand-new style of muscular American feminism," the author Camille Paglia wrote in the London *Times* on September 14, 2008. "At her startling debut at the Republican convention, she was combining male and female qualities in ways that I have never seen before. And she was somehow able to seem simultaneously reassuringly traditional and gung-ho futurist. In terms of redefining the persona for female authority and leadership, Palin has made the biggest step forward in feminism since Madonna channeled the dominatrix persona of high-glam Marlene Dietrich and rammed pro-sex, pro-beauty feminism down the throats of the prissy, victim-mongering, philistine feminist establishment." Say what you will about Paglia, but she does not mince words.

Few self-described feminists shared Paglia's enthusiasm for Palin. But the brilliant and eccentric cultural analyst always has been unafraid to speak her mind, especially when she disagrees with prevailing opinion (which is often). Paglia's essays defending Palin were important because they acknowledged that Palin was a real woman, not a pretender, with her own brand of femininity and feminism that deserved recognition. For Paglia, Palin was a character from America's past. "She immediately reminded me of the frontier women of the western states, which first granted women the right to vote after the Civil War—long before the federal amendment guaranteeing universal suffrage was passed in 1919," she wrote. "Frontier women faced the same harsh challenges and had to tackle the same chores as men, which is why men could regard them as equals—unlike the genteel, corseted ladies of the eastern seaboard." Palin's familiarity and comfort with guns, her Alaskan heritage, and her frenetic family and professional life all reinforced Paglia's comparison.

One does not have to agree with all of Paglia's analysis to acknowledge that Palin truly represented something new. Until she appeared, the most prominent women in American politics were either past the age at which they could bear children (Geraldine Ferraro, Hillary Clinton, Madeleine Albright, and Nancy Pelosi) or deliberately de-emphasized their sex as they jostled for influence over powerful men (Janet Reno, Condoleezza Rice, Janet Napolitano). The spokeswomen for the feminist establishment were all on the left, serving as one of the most powerful interests in the Democratic Party and a monolithic bloc of opinion on America's college campuses. And the most influential Republican women—Rice, Christine Todd Whitman, Kay Bailey Hutchison, and Meg Whitman, for example—were all pro-choice. The women at the highest reaches of our political, economic, and cultural life shared great wealth, status, and power. This wasn't exactly surprising; after all, they were at the pinnacle of their careers. But riches and glory did separate them from the large majority of American women.

Then Palin showed up. At forty-four, she was still young. She was fertile, having just delivered her fifth child a few months before her debut. She was fetching. She did not think society had victimized her. She spoke like an ordinary person. She was decidedly unpretentious. She had not been educated at America's elite universities. She had never studied abroad. She faced challenges like everybody else. Her parents were neither famous nor rich. She had not married into wealth. Her family required two working parents to make ends meet. She had to deal with a pregnant teenage daughter and a newborn son with Down syndrome. She was unabashedly pro-life. She made no apologies for what she thought, said, and did.

It is hard to measure the galvanic effect Palin had on many women, Republican women in particular. Women as a whole were more inclined to like Palin before the feral beast went after her, but even after the 2008 election, many women who disagreed with Palin's politics nonetheless sympathized with her plight.

For Republican and conservative women, however, Palin has remained a powerful figure. When you attended a Palin rally during the campaign, you were struck most by the number of women who had brought their daughters to catch a glimpse of the vice presidential candidate. Palin made it acceptable, even glamorous, to be a conservative woman. Many women who might have felt cut off from grievance-based adversarial feminism could look to her as an alternative. Meanwhile, mothers of disabled children had also found an advocate. Perhaps most important, women in a variety of economic and social circumstances could identify with her normality and struggles.

This was a monumental opportunity to disrupt the received narrative of American feminism. Palin attempted to take the banner of feminism from the likes of Gloria Steinem and Cintra Wilson, and expand it to include conservative women as well as liberals, lower-middle-class mothers as well as college-educated ones. Her brand of feminism is syncretic. She is a forceful advocate for Title IX, the legislation that ties school funding to gender equality. But she also says high taxes hurt small-business women and calls for a family-friendly tax code and laws to help working moms who want to spend more time at home.

Palin's October 21, 2008, policy speech on women's issues in Henderson, Nevada, played the gender card when she accused Barack Obama of not paying his female Senate staffers equal pay for equal work. She said that Obama's denial of the vice presidency to Hillary Clinton was another example of the glass ceiling blocking women from promotion. She advocated a broad, forceful, universalist American foreign policy to promote women's rights that Clinton herself would probably be comfortable supporting.

"Across the world," Palin said that day, "there are still places where women are subjugated and persecuted, as they were in Afghanistan, places where they're bullied and brutalized and murdered in honor killings, places where women are sold like commodities in the nightmare world of the sex trade, and places where baby girls are unwelcome as a matter of state policy and their mothers are forced to have abortions." Her job as vice president, she went on, would be to fight for all women in the hopes that such injustices were redressed.

Palin's speech in Henderson was not only a rebuke to those who said she was unconcerned with policy. It was also the governor's first major attempt to articulate the principles behind, and the policy implications of, her independent, self-made, frontier feminism. In a fair world, the address would have received far more coverage than it did. But the world is not fair. The day after Palin's speech, Politico broke the news that the Republican National Committee had spent more than $150,000 on wardrobe for the Palins. Guess which story dominated the headlines.

THE RULES OF ATTRACTION

Palin's attractiveness heightened the tension between perceptions of her femininity and evaluations of her competence. The University of South

Florida psychologists Nathan Heflick and Jamie Goldenberg have found that subjects judge highly attractive women less competent for top positions. Their article "Objectifying Sarah Palin," published in the May 2009 issue of the *Journal of Experimental Social Psychology*, hypothesizes that "focusing on a woman's appearance will promote reduced perceptions of competence, and also, by virtue of construing the woman as an 'object,' perceptions of the woman as less human."

The authors include some empirical evidence to back an argument that is more or less self-evident. Practically everybody has noticed, at one time or another, that good-looking people get favorable treatment because other, not-so-good-looking people want to curry favor with them. When it comes to intellectual matters or executive management, though, the situation is reversed. In these arenas, where the brainiacs rule, beautiful women must prove they have substance. They must demonstrate that they are not "dumb blondes" or "bimbos," or are somehow trading on their good looks.

Comely women face a tough climb. In Sarah Palin's case, a governor who had tamed the oil companies, reformed Alaska's government, and enjoyed sky-high approval ratings was reduced to a sex object. A series of photo hoaxes circulated on the Web purporting to reveal Palin in sexually provocative dress. One showed Palin wearing an American flag bikini and holding a rifle at a pool party. Another showed Palin leaning against a kitchen counter, wearing a black miniskirt, high heels, and a low-cut blue top. A Chinese-language newspaper went so far as to publish what it said was a nude photo of Palin. All these images were fakes. And yet the power of these photographs was in the way they stripped Palin—in the case of the Chinese newspaper, literally—of her personality, biography, and politics. They removed her from any context. They shrank Palin to manageable size. After all, Americans are used to viewing titillating photographs of beautiful women. We are not used to having beautiful women in positions of great power. Falsely conveying the idea that Palin was just another entrant in *Maxim* magazine's "Hometown Hotties" contest was a way to assert authority over her.

"Everybody has strong reactions to pretty women," Michael Goldfarb said. "People either loved [Palin] or they hated her, and I think her looks had something to do with it." The left, for its part, did its best to suggest that Palin's sexuality was somehow threatening. On September 12, 2008, the liberal radio talk-show host Randi Rhodes said of Palin, "She's friends with all the teenage boys. You have to say no when your kids go, 'Can we sleep over at the Palins?' No! No!" A slide show on GQ.com referred to Palin as the "cougar in chief," and added that "the first dude will not be the only man she'll leave her paw prints on." Such baseless intimations of promiscuity reinforced the impression that Palin was nothing more than a sexual object, and the most disturbing kind: aggressive.

Another argument was that Palin's attractiveness could harm the country overtly, by scandal and unbridled eros, or covertly, by clouding male opinions of her. McCain, it was said, had not been listening to his brain when he asked Palin to join the GOP ticket. On September 2, 2008, for example, another liberal radio talk-show host, Stephanie Miller, said McCain introduced "his trophy VP before he stepped back to check out her a** for twenty minutes." Then a McCain impersonator on the show chimed in, saying, "The middle part of 'Alaska' is a** . . . and she's got a terrific one, my friends. She puts the a** in Alaska."

In a September 17, 2008, radio commentary, a former Republican senator from Minnesota, David Durenberger, said that "Sarah Palin didn't blink when John McCain asked her to marry him on their second date." Tony Norman of the *Pittsburgh Post-Gazette* wrote on October 7, 2008, that "from an early age, she knew the power of a strategically placed hand on the bicep of some jock. Girls like Sarah Palin knew how to secure a place with the 'in crowd.' After all, she was the girl with the iridescent smile who provided the laugh track for the meatheads roaming the halls pulling wedgies on those who would never qualify as 'their kind of people.'"

In an October 24, 2008, article, syndicated columnist Kathleen Parker suggested that McCain had picked Palin to be his running mate because "his judgment may have been clouded by" the governor's appearance. The happy accident of Palin's attractiveness was consistently held against her. In a September 23, 2008, *Huffington Post* blog, novelist Valerie Frankel wrote that "[d]ue to her Miss Alaska runner-up credentials, Palin has enjoyed a life, thus far, of getting what she wants, whenever she wants it, regardless of rules, consequences, and fairness."

The subtle negation of Palin's capacity and talent, the attribution of her entire career and impact to her good looks, was a classic illustration of Kathleen Hall Jamieson's double bind. When Palin visited the United Nations in September 2008, the trip was likened to nothing more than an American courting ritual. CNN correspondent Ed Henry said on Anderson Cooper's show that Palin's trip amounted to "speed dating with world leaders." That same day, the German writer Michael Knigge wrote on Deutsche Welle's Across the Pond blog that Palin's meetings were "a political speed dating effort." The major news story from Palin's meetings at the U.N. was that the Pakistani president, Asif Ali Zardari, called the vice presidential candidate "gorgeous" and admitted he "might hug" her. Zardari's comments were not serious. His words did not warrant serious coverage. But since they fed into the media storyline that Palin was something akin to a Republican Barbie doll, they were trumpeted all over the airwaves.

Palin's bearing so unsettled liberals that they took care to insult her looks whenever they had the chance. Heather Mallick wrote on the Web site of the Canadian Broadcasting Corporation that "Palin has a toned-down version of the porn actress look." At one point in her Salon piece, Cintra Wilson called Palin a "Republican blow-up doll." The editor-in-chief of the *New Republic,* Martin Peretz, wrote on his blog on September 4, 2008, that Palin was "pretty like a cosmetics saleswoman at Macy's" and asked God to "rescue us from these swilly people." In a September 20, 2008, article, *New York Times* columnist Maureen Dowd likened Palin to a "Lancôme rep who thinks *The Flintstones* was based on a true story." Appearing on *The View* on September 30, 2008, Bill Maher called Palin a "bimbo." In 2009 David Letterman would compare Palin to a "slutty flight attendant" and an "Applebee's waitress."

Meanwhile, Palin's likeness was being exploited for demeaning purposes. In October 2008, the adult-novelty business Topco released the This is Not Sarah Palin Inflatable Love Doll. The press release announcing the product launch said, "The sexy 'This is Not Sarah Palin Inflatable Love Doll' won't debate you—and that's a good thing." Feminist writer Susannah Breslin didn't find the doll disgusting, though. Palin and Gloria Steinem, Breslin wrote on Slate.com's "The XX Factor" blog on October 21, 2008, are "both as aware of their sexuality as they are dead-set on focusing on politics over sex, but how can we be surprised when Americans respond in kind and sexualize the images of those women whose sexual complexities sit center stage in American politics?"

This Alfred E. Neuman, "What, Me Worry?" reaction signaled that feminists grew a thick skin whenever they discussed slights to Sarah Palin—but *only* then. For them, sliming Palin by turning her into a sex toy was no big deal. Nor was Hustler Video's production of *Who's Nailin' Paylin* [*sic*], a hardcore pornographic movie starring adult film star Lisa Ann as "Serra Paylin," who engages in numerous sex acts (at least according to Wikipedia!) with actors portraying Russian soldiers as well as actresses made up as Hillary Clinton and Condoleezza Rice. The film

was successful enough to have launched a sequel: *Obama Is Nailin'*
Paylin. Then, in yet another sign of the collapse of the American moral
consensus and the mainstreaming of pornographic imagery, Lisa Ann
became famous for her Palin "impression" and appeared, among other
places, in an Eminem music video in 2009.

The Palin "love doll" and Hustler's pornos were fundamental expressions of male power over women. "[P]ornography is, and always
has been, a man's work," Irving Kristol wrote in his 1971 essay "Pornography, Obscenity and the Case for Censorship." "[W]hatever the
explanation, there can be no question that pornography is a form of
'sexism,' as the women's liberation movement calls it, and that the instinct of women's liberation has been unerring in perceiving that when
pornography is perpetrated, it is perpetrated against them, as part of a
conspiracy to deprive them of their full humanity."

The "instinct of women's liberation" did err, however, when Sarah
Palin was the target. The press covered the sex stories with no editorial
comment. If anything, the blow-up doll and direct-to-video smut were
portrayed as just two more entries in the free-flowing, wild-and-crazy
carnival of American erotica. And while a few women did speak out,
they were few and far between. Palin critic Marie Cocco wrote in the
October 2, 2008, *Asbury Park Press* that objectifying the governor was
"a terrible predicament not only for Palin but for all American women."
Camille Paglia and conservative hero Phyllis Schlafly also decried the
harsh and insensitive treatment undergone by Palin. Not once, though,
did traditional feminists rally to Palin's defense. The love doll and porno
were two plain-as-day examples of the sexual double standard that
women confront on a daily basis. Has a male political figure ever been
similarly sexualized, objectified, and dehumanized? Yet the reaction
from those who would normally protest was . . . silence.

PALIN AND ANTI-PALIN

The announcer's voice was crisp and even-keeled. "And now a nonpartisan message from Governor Sarah Palin and Senator Hillary Clinton," he said, as the camera faded in on a wooden lectern in front of a blue curtain and four American flags. Sarah Palin and Hillary Clinton stood side by side, Palin in a red jacket and black skirt, Clinton in a blue top and jacket and black slacks. But these women were actually comediennes Tina Fey and Amy Poehler impersonating Palin and Clinton. The show was *Saturday Night Live*. This wasn't reality. It was a joke.

The difference may have been lost on a lot of viewers. When Fey debuted her Palin impression on September 13, 2008, the female comic altered the landscape of the presidential race. The fact that Fey and Palin resemble each other so closely added gravity to the actress's caricature. The audience loved every second of it. According to the trade periodical *Advertising Age, SNL* ratings jumped by 76 percent thanks to Fey's impersonation, and NBC.com recorded 27.7 million views of skits featuring Fey as Palin. And when Palin herself appeared on the show on October 18, 2008, Nielsen recorded the highest overnight rating for *SNL* since 1994. Palin was good for business.

If Lisa Ann's "performances" conveyed the message that Sarah Palin was no more than a sex object, Tina Fey's lent the impression that Palin was simply a happy-go-lucky idiot. Fey took Palin's regional, non-Mid-Atlantic accent and exaggerated it to make Palin seem exotic and out of touch. She minced and posed like the beauty pageant contestant that Palin had been decades ago. Whenever Fey's Palin character faced a dilemma, or just had to fill time, she drew attention to her good looks. The overall effect was to make Palin seem lightweight, stupid, and out of her league. In one skit, Fey's Palin and Will Ferrell's George W. Bush got along famously, two doltish yokels from unfashionable locales hamming it up. In another, the superficiality of Fey's Palin was juxtaposed with the substance of Poehler's Clinton. There was no hint that Palin was a successful governor who had worked with both parties and enjoyed widespread support.

A television show like *Saturday Night Live* reaches an audience that does not pay close attention to politics. Thus, Fey's impersonation held tremendous power. It became difficult for many to determine where the fake Palin ended and the real Palin began. The Palin caricature was a means by which myths about the vice presidential candidate infiltrated the public consciousness. Consider that first sketch. In it, Poehler's Hillary Clinton says that global warming is a threat, whereas Fey's Palin says climate change is "just God huggin' us closer." This was the show's way of emphasizing the false notion that Palin does not think mankind may play a role in global warming. (Palin to Charlie Gibson, September 11, 2008: "I'm attributing some of man's activities to potentially causing some of the changes in the climate right now.") Later in the skit, Poehler's Clinton gestures to Fey's Palin and says, "Ask this one about dinosaurs," another implicit reference to an already tired lie about the governor.

Most famously, the September 13, 2008, skit included the moment when Fey's Palin said, "And I can see Russia from my house." The line encapsulated what liberals saw as Palin's stupidity and provinciality. Palin had never said anything like it, however. She had told interviewers that you can see Russia from Alaska, which is accurate. But the Fey line stuck, as it was repeated over and over on news broadcasts and the Internet. Later, when the documentarian and radio talk show host John Ziegler commissioned a Zogby poll of Obama voters for *Media Malpractice,* he found that whereas more than 70 percent of respondents were unaware Joe Biden had quit an earlier presidential campaign due to plagiarism, a stunning 86.9 percent believed the Russia line sprang from Palin's own lips.

It was telling that Fey should be the actress who impersonated Palin. The two women may look like each other, but they could not be more dissimilar. Each exemplifies a different category of feminism. Palin comes from the I-can-do-it-all school. She is professionally successful, has been married for more than twenty years, and has a large and (from all outward appearances) happy family. And while Fey is also pretty, married, and has a daughter, the characters she portrays in films like *Mean Girls* and *Baby Mama,* and in television shows like *30 Rock,* are hard-pressed eggheads who give up personal fulfillment—e.g., marriage and motherhood—in the pursuit of professional success. On *30 Rock,* Fey, who is also the show's chief writer and executive producer, plays Liz Lemon, a television comedy writer modeled on herself. Liz Lemon is smart, funny, and at the top of her field. But she fails elsewhere. None of her relationships with men works out. She wants desperately to raise a child but can find neither the time nor the means to marry or adopt. Lemon makes you laugh, for sure. But you also would be hard pressed to name a more unhappy person on American television.

Palin's sudden global fame rankled those feminists whose own path to glory had been difficult. To them, Palin was less a female success story than she was the beneficiary of male chauvinism. To them, Palin's physical and personal appeal had done more to carry her upward than her intelligence and canniness. Palin's personal contentedness and conservative beliefs only poured salt on this feminist wound. That Palin seemed unconcerned with what her opponents thought of her was more frustrating still. Maureen Dowd obsessed over Palin and seemed to delight in ridiculing her, calling the governor any number of names and reducing a unique woman to a cartoon. This was not surprising. Dowd, like Fey, preaches an ascetic feminism in which marriage and family are obstacles to female success and happiness—in 2005, for instance, she published a book titled *Are Men Necessary?*

In their politics, backgrounds, attitudes, and antagonisms, Fey and Dowd are anti-Palins. They used comedy to assert superiority over the upstart from Alaska whose prominence and success challenged their core beliefs.

And this was the context in which Palin's interviews with CBS News anchor Katie Couric took place.

THE COURIC FILE

It was a lousy interview.

Palin's dislike for Couric was obvious. After the first day's taping was finished, she did not want to sit down with Couric twice more. Palin says she has not watched the finished interview to this day. Looking back, it is something of a mystery why the McCain campaign decided to give the governor's second televised interview as the GOP vice presidential nominee to a broadcaster known for her hostility to conservatives. Perhaps the choice had something to do with Palin handler Nicolle Wallace's friendship with Couric and her association with CBS News. Perhaps the McCain high command wanted to punish NBC for the incredibly hostile and slanted coverage of its sister cable network MSNBC.

Whatever the reason, at the end of September 2008, Palin found herself confronted with a series of interviews to be broadcast on a network that just four years earlier had trumpeted forged documents as "evidence" that George W. Bush had performed inadequately in the Air National Guard in the 1970s. Couric was given unprecedented access. She interviewed the governor solo several times and spoke to McCain and Palin together once. The feast of material, spread over three different nights, would surely help Couric's ratings. The McCain campaign was doing her a favor.

Couric did not return the favor, however. The bias in her questions was clear. "Other than supporting stricter regulations of Fannie Mae and Freddie Mac two years ago, can you give us any more examples of [John McCain's] leading the charge for more oversight?" she asked Palin. The question was rigged. Couric removed from consideration one of McCain's selling points: he had worked to impose restrictions on mortgage giants Fannie and Freddie while the Democrats, Barack Obama included, looked the other way. With that off of the table, of course Palin couldn't come up with any other "examples of his leading the charge for more oversight" or regulation. On the whole, the man supports free markets.

When the topic was foreign policy, Couric asked Palin: "You met yesterday with former secretary of State Henry Kissinger, who is for direct diplomacy with both Iran and Syria. Do you believe the U.S. should negotiate with leaders like President Assad and Ahmadinejad?" Palin said Obama's pledge to meet with rogue dictators was "naïve," and Couric pounced. "Are you saying Henry Kissinger is naïve for supporting that?" she said. Couric was obliterating the distinction between Kissinger's preferred policy—direct negotiations from a position of strength—and Obama's—presidential meetings with tyrants without preconditions. Palin correctly called her on it. "I've never heard Henry Kissinger say, 'Yeah, I'll meet with these leaders without preconditions being met,'" she said.

Couric asked Palin probing questions as to why she had not had a passport before 2007, whether she thought global warming was man-made, whether she supported contraception and the morning-after pill, why the United States shouldn't "second-guess" Israel, why one of her churches hosted a group that said homosexuality could be cured through prayer, and whether she was qualified to be vice president. Fine. Reporters should ask tough questions. Politicians should be prepared to answer them. And yet, when one compares Couric's tough questions to Palin with what the news anchor subsequently asked Joe Biden, the Palin interrogatory seems more partisan than journalistic. For example, Couric asked Biden: "Have you found that you have to be über-careful and disciplined in terms of being out there on the campaign trail?" And: "How is it preparing for the debates?" And: "Are you worried that you're going to have to pull your punches a bit because of her gender and you don't want to seem like you're bullying her?" (This was not a problem for Couric.) The Biden interview was all softballs. The Palin interview was change-ups, splitters, knuckle balls, and curves.

The Couric interview cannot be properly evaluated without first considering the circumstances in which it occurred. Couric talked to Palin as the global economy teetered on the edge of collapse. The bankruptcy of the investment bank Lehman Brothers on September 15, 2008, shook asset prices and froze credit markets. While the economy had been in recession since December 2007, September 2008 was the moment when it verged on a depression. No one knew what to do. The day after Lehman went under, the federal government effectively nationalized the global insurance giant AIG. Soon thereafter, panicked policy makers at the Treasury Department and the Federal Reserve began urging Congress to pass the Troubled Asset Relief Program (TARP), a $700-billion-plus emergency bank bailout that would allow the government to purchase toxic assets from major financial institutions. Global economic anxiety blossomed into a full-bore financial and political panic.

The causes of the economic crisis were complicated. The deflation of artificially high housing prices led to the insolvency of overleveraged financial institutions that had incorrectly wagered that real estate values would go up forever. The banks' plunging bottom lines led to a freeze in commercial and personal lending, which in turn led to plummeting consumer demand and widespread unemployment. Just as complicated as the roots of the problem were the potential solutions. The TARP might have been necessary to forestall a breakdown in the global financial system, but it was hard to explain that to Americans who were increasingly out of work and who blamed the banks for the economy's troubles. The drama and dread of the moment made a lot of Republican economic doctrines look anachronistic.

When Palin accepted John McCain's offer to be his running mate, no one could have known that in less than a month the international financial system would be on the brink. Palin's appeal was cultural, her main issue was energy, and the McCain team had done its best to fight the campaign on national security grounds. As soon as Lehman imploded, however, the campaign's assumptions were all overturned. The 2008 election would be decided on which candidate could best navigate choppy economic waters.

Moreover, while Palin had been extensively briefed on foreign policy, and could speak with ease on Iran, Afghanistan, and Russia, she did not display a fine grasp of McCain's domestic agenda. That may have been because there wasn't much of a McCain domestic agenda to begin with; especially after the crisis hit, McCain was making things up as he went along. Even so, Couric was there to exploit the gap in Palin's knowledge. "Couric made it very clear early on that she had an agenda," John Ziegler told me.

Regarding the TARP, Couric asked Palin, Why isn't it better to spend $700 billion on people who are struggling with health care and grocery bills? The answer to this question, which McCain and Obama perfected on the stump, was that without a banking system no one would have a job and health care. Therefore, as distasteful a policy as it may be, the government had to bail out the goons who had gotten us into this mess in the first place. It was clear from her response to Couric's question that Palin wanted to say something similar. What came out of her mouth, however, was a grab bag of platitudes: "Not necessarily [TARP], as it's been proposed, has to pass or we're going to find ourselves in another Great Depression. But there has got to be action—bipartisan effort—Congress not pointing fingers at one another but finding the solution to this, taking action, and being serious about the reforms on Wall Street that are needed." Later Palin did her best to tie the bailout to health care and job creation, but didn't make her point coherently. It was her worst moment of the campaign.

There were plenty of other moments during the interview when Palin should have known better. Her refusal to answer Couric's question about which newspapers she read regularly was Palin's way of telling the broadcaster to go jump in a lake, but that was not the way viewers interpreted it. What's more, her inability to identify a Supreme Court decision other than *Roe v. Wade* with which she disagreed was baffling, since she had publicly criticized the Court's decision in *Exxon Shipping Co. v. Baker* only a few months before.

Palin's interview with Couric was probably the most damaging to a politician's credibility since 1979, when Ted Kennedy found himself unable to tell CBS's Roger Mudd why he wanted to be president. The media made sure that Palin's bad moments received maximum exposure. Tina Fey broke out her Sarah Palin character again, this time with Poehler portraying Couric, and played up Palin's inability to describe the logic behind the TARP. On *Late Edition* on September 28, CNN anchor Wolf Blitzer showed clips from the Couric interview back-to-back with an excerpt from Fey's parody. In the background, you can hear the show's panelists laugh at Fey's spoof. To the chattering class, Palin had always been a joke. Now they thought they had evidence.

One bad interview does not ruin a candidacy or a career, however. "It was tough," a senior Palin aide said of the Couric experience. "It wasn't fun. But incidents like that became exaggerated because they were so high-profile." Sure enough, Palin recovered her footing quickly.

For their part, of course, Palin's opponents in the media took the Couric interview as confirmation that the governor was toast. Naturally, they have a tendency to overestimate the power of the media. What passed for consensus among the media elite was thought to be the only considered and justifiable opinion plausible. And because the interview was Palin's worst, Couric's fellow reporters celebrated her "scoop." After the election, Couric won the Edward R. Murrow Award for Best Newscast, the Walter Cronkite Award for Special Achievement in Journalism, the Helen Thomas Award for Excellence in Journalism, the American Women in Radio and Television's Gracie Allen Award, and the Al Neuharth Award for Excellence in the Media. The media made no pretense as to the reason for the accolades. In May 2009, at the gala dinner in Washington where Couric received the Helen Thomas Award—with former Palin campaign aide Nicolle Wallace in attendance—the grizzled Thomas pronounced from the lectern that Couric had "the right stuff to do that game-changing interview" with Palin and thereby "saved the country." The audience gave Thomas a standing ovation.

Chapter Seven
The Classless Media: The Elite's Condescending Attitude Toward Ordinary Americans

THE name was giving her trouble.

As September turned into October 2008, Palin spent three days at John McCain's ranch in Sedona, Arizona, preparing for her October 2 debate with Joe Biden. The beautiful scenery was the backdrop for intense preparation and rehearsal. The McCain team wanted to make the experience as comfortable as possible for Palin. To that end, the campaign staff ensured that Todd Palin, with the couple's three youngest children in tow, accompanied the governor to the ranch. McCain strategist Mark McKinnon, who had left the campaign in June rather than work against Barack Obama, also traveled to Sedona to give Palin advice. The two hit it off. Palin's most trusted aide, her friend Kris Perry, came too. Perry had been marooned in Alaska, dealing with the fallout from the Troopergate inquiry. Other campaign aides told me that Perry's separation from Palin during the tumultuous month of September had intensified whatever anxiety the governor was feeling at the time.

The stress was understandable. When she joined the Republican ticket, Palin had been plucked from her Alaska team and catapulted into a foreign campaign apparatus. She had no prior relationship with her campaign chief of staff, her campaign handlers, her speechwriters, or her campaign spokeswoman. She couldn't help feeling disoriented. Having Todd Palin and Kris Perry close by gave her ballast as she readied for her high-profile showdown with the six-term senator from Delaware.

Palin had never met Biden and did not know what to expect. Luckily, during the mock debates at Sedona, McCain foreign policy adviser Randy Scheunemann played Obama's running mate. Scheunemann's portrayal was so canny, Palin later remarked, that she was a little taken aback when she met the real Biden on stage.

When rehearsals began, Palin started well. After she and Scheunemann finished the first run-through, there was spontaneous applause. "She did wonderfully," one participant in the session told me. There were a few hiccups, however. The major one was that Palin kept referring to her opponent as "Senator O'Biden." No one wanted the verbal slip to distract from Palin's performance. Eventually the team arrived at a potential solution: call him Joe. That way the problematic last name would be avoided altogether.

So, a few days later, when Palin walked out onto the stage at Washington University in St. Louis to meet Joe Biden and shake his hand, the world watched as she leaned forward and asked him, "Hey, can I call you Joe?"

Biden agreed, and the two were off.

The name gambit worked, for the most part. During the debate, Palin did make a passing reference to the imaginary "Senator O'Biden." But only once. Her other mistakes also involved names. She twice referred to then-NATO commander in Afghanistan, General David McKiernan, as General "McClellan."

Other than these three slips of the tongue, however, Palin made no major gaffes in the course of the ninety-minute debate. Yes, on occasion she did shade the truth—but so did Biden. What politician doesn't? On the whole, her performance was remarkable for a novice. Palin was composed, direct, and appealing. She achieved several things. She asserted her credentials without, as she put it, "the filter, even, of the mainstream media kind of telling viewers what they've just heard." She effectively severed the Bush years from the 2008 GOP ticket, treating the Bush presidency as an object for historical inquiry and not political debate. She did her best to marry the McCain-Palin pledge of reform to the real concerns of everyday Americans.

"I think a good barometer here," she said, "as we try to figure out has this been a good time or a bad time in America's economy, is go to a kid's soccer game on Saturday, and turn to any parent there on the sideline and ask them, 'How are you feeling about the economy?'" In the midst of the financial panic, Palin had no problem bashing the banking class. "Darn right it was the predatory lenders," she said in response to a question about "who was at fault" for the mortgage troubles. Nor did she have any illusions as to whose side she was on: "Let's commit ourselves, just everyday American people, Joe Six Pack, hockey moms across the nation, I think we need to band together and say 'never again.'" Her colloquial speech, non–East Coast accent, casual manner, and relatable background bolstered her argument for solidarity.

Both candidates presented themselves as champions of a neglected middle class. Biden uttered the phrase "middle class" twelve times. He pledged that the Obama economic program would "focus on the middle class" because "when the middle class is growing, the economy grows and everybody does well, not just focus on the wealthy and corporate America." He evoked his hardscrabble roots on the streets of Scranton, Pennsylvania. "You know," Biden said, "in the neighborhood

I grew up in, it was all about dignity and respect. A neighborhood like most of you grew up in. And in that neighborhood, it was filled with women and men, mothers and fathers who taught their children if they believed in themselves, if they were honest, if they worked hard, if they loved their country, they could accomplish anything."

For Biden, the major consequence of center-right governments since Ronald Reagan (including, in hindsight, Bill Clinton's) was the immolation of such neighborhoods and the erosion of such teachings. According to this view, a different sort of economic program—one involving higher taxes on upper-income earners, universal health care, policies designed to benefit Big Labor, and more government spending on education and the environment—would restore the American middle class to the status it enjoyed around, say, 1965, before the crime wave, the flight from the cities, the breakdown of Keynesian economics under Nixon and Carter, the onset of globalization, and the dislocations of the information economy.

If Biden spoke for middle-class economic interests, Palin spoke for middle-class cultural identity. But she also pointed out that the Obama ticket preferred "solutions" to perceived middle-class decline that wouldn't necessarily improve anybody's economic condition. "We can speak in agreement here that darn right we need tax relief for Americans so that jobs can be created here," Palin said. "Barack Obama even supported increasing taxes as late as last year for those families making only forty-two thousand dollars a year. That's a lot of middle-income average American families to increase taxes on them. I think that is the way to kill jobs and to continue to harm our economy."

In Palin's view, Obama's national health insurance program also carried potential drawbacks. "Barack Obama's plan is to mandate health care coverage and have [a] universal government-run program," she said, "and unless you're pleased with the way the federal government has been running anything lately, I don't think that it's going to be real pleasing for Americans to consider health care being taken over by the feds."

It did not help Biden that many of the stories he told during the debate were fictional. He committed gaffe after gaffe, at some moments layering the mistruths on top of one another so thickly that it became impossible to disentangle them. At one point on October 2, Biden said, "When we kicked—along with France, we kicked Hezbollah out of Lebanon, I said and Barack said, 'Move NATO forces in there. Fill the vacuum, because if you don't know—if you don't, Hezbollah will control it.'"

What was he saying? Neither "we" nor France ever kicked Hezbollah out of Lebanon. As of this writing, it's part of the government there. Biden also said, "Our commanding general in Afghanistan said the surge principle in Iraq will not work in Afghanistan." Sorry. As Palin pointed out, General McKiernan did not quite say that. True, he told the *Washington Post* on October 2 that "Afghanistan is not Iraq" and the "word I don't use for Afghanistan is 'surge.'" But during the same interview he also called for a "sustained [American] commitment" to Afghanistan, a counterinsurgency strategy, and additional forces—all of which are elements of the surge. Indeed, in the spring of 2009, the Obama White House would later adopt—against Biden's counsel—a strategy in Afghanistan similar to General Petraeus's surge strategy in Iraq.

Biden said, "We spend more money in three weeks on combat in Iraq than we spent on the entirety of the last seven years that we have been in Afghanistan." But, as Carl Cannon noted in a July 8, 2009, article on PoliticsDaily.com, "The facts here were that at the time Biden was speaking, the U.S. had spent $172 billion in Afghanistan. The Iraq war consumes between $7 billion and $8 billion every three weeks. Biden's math was off by two thousand percent."

Speaking of the man he'd hoped to replace, Dick Cheney, Biden said, "The idea he doesn't realize that Article I of the Constitution defines the role of the vice president of the United States, that's the Executive Branch." The idea that Joe Biden, a sometime constitutional law professor at a university in Delaware, didn't realize that Article I of the Constitution deals with the legislative branch is troubling. According to Biden, moreover, Barack Obama "did not say [he'd] sit down with Ahmadinejad." That is exactly what Obama said, however, at the CNN YouTube debate in July 2007. Biden even criticized Obama for saying it at the time.

In his debate with Palin, Biden claimed that John McCain opposed intervention in Bosnia. Untrue. Despite being an early skeptic of American involvement in the Balkans, McCain stood by President Clinton's peacekeeping mission there and later became a forceful advocate for war against Serbian aggression in Kosovo. Biden said that McCain voted against "a Comprehensive Nuclear Test Ban Treaty that every Republican has supported." McCain did vote against the treaty, but he wasn't alone. Fifty other GOP senators voted with him. Biden said that McCain "voted the exact same way" as Obama on a budget resolution that included tax hikes beginning in 2011. Nope. McCain wasn't there for the vote.

In his PoliticsDaily.com piece, Carl Cannon caught Biden in another whopper that hasn't received much attention. "Pakistan already has deployed nuclear weapons," Biden said. "Pakistan's weapons can already hit Israel and the Mediterranean." But, as Cannon noted, "Pakistan has no known intercontinental missiles. The range of its weapons is thought to be one thousand miles—halfway to Israel." Finally, toward the end of the debate, Biden urged the audience to "go down Union Street with me in Wilmington, or go to Katie's Restaurant, or walk into Home Depot with me where I spend a lot of time" to see the harm the Bush administration had inflicted on the economy. How much time Biden spends in Home Depot is his own business, but Katie's Restaurant has been closed for nearly thirty years.

The exemplary Biden misstatement happened during his interview with Katie Couric, when he told his interlocutor that "when the stock market crashed, Franklin D. Roosevelt got on the television and didn't just talk about the, you know, the princes of greed. He said, 'Look, here's what happened.'"

This was so untrue it was almost funny. The stock market crashed in 1929. Herbert Hoover, not Franklin D. Roosevelt, was president. And when he became president in 1933, Roosevelt did not get "on the television." Such technology was primitive back then. FDR's medium was radio. On top of that, you'd be hard pressed to find FDR singling out the "princes of greed." He went after "plutocrats" and "economic royalists"; his cousin Theodore attacked the "malefactors of great wealth." Biden had no idea what he was talking about.

If Sarah Palin had made a similar assertion, she would have been tarred and feathered as a dope who had no place in politics. When Biden said it, though, Democrats and the press laughed it off, saying, "That's just Joe." Exactly. That's just Joe being a fool.

Biden's gaffes did not cease once he became vice president. On the day he and Obama were inaugurated, Biden said, "Jill and I had the great honor of standing on that stage" that morning, "looking across at one of the great justices, Justice Stewart." Stewart died a quarter century ago. Speaking to administration supporters on February 6, 2009, Biden said, "If we do everything right, if we do it with absolute certainty, there's still a thirty percent chance we're going to get it wrong." And in April 2009, as the White House worked to prevent a panic over an outbreak of swine flu, Biden said on the *Today* show that he "wouldn't go anywhere in confined places," including airplanes and subways. "That's me," he said, as though the vice president's opinion, publicly expressed, carried no real weight. The White House had to disavow Biden's outburst—an activity that they have become accustomed to doing.

Joe Biden's foot is in his mouth so often it's a wonder the rest of us can make out what he's saying (and saying and saying). The man is a national embarrassment. Biden may have a friendly demeanor, and those who know him well say he is a genuinely nice person, but his record on national security—his signature issue—is sketchy at best. In the 1980s, he opposed the Reagan Doctrine and the Strategic Defense Initiative. In 1991 he opposed expelling Saddam Hussein from Kuwait. In 2002 he voted to invade Iraq in order to disarm Saddam, only to disavow his vote when the Iraqi civil war spun out of control. In 2007 he strenuously opposed the surge. Then, when the surge in Iraq worked, he argued against the attempt to implement a similar policy in Afghanistan. Despite all this, however, the former ambassador to Morocco Marc Ginsberg wrote on the *Huffington Post* on August 29, 2008, that "[P]utting Sarah Palin into a debate with Joe Biden is going to be like throwing Howdy Doody into a knife fight!"

Howdy Doody must have brought along a machete and a couple of broadswords, because Sarah Palin went toe-to-toe with Biden, the consummate Beltway insider, a fixture on the cable chat circuit for years, and gave as good as—if not better than—she got. She was collected, attractive, down to earth, and confident. She made no big slips. Yet the unanimous decision of the political press corps was that *Biden* won the vice presidential debate. Why?

DEMOCRACY AND MERITOCRACY

Part of the answer has to do with partisanship. Palin would have had to deal a knockout blow to Biden for the media to acknowledge her win.

She didn't do that. She fought Biden to a draw. This was too complicated a result for the media to certify, as their rule book states that any
ambiguity in outcome is immediately scored for Barack Obama. Hence,
Biden was crowned the victor.

Yet there was also something larger than partisanship at work. The
reason the press corps took Biden more seriously than Palin had a lot
to do with the class structure. This is not to say that Palin got a raw deal
because her annual income is lower than Joe Biden's—in fact, Biden
was one of the poorest members of the Senate. Nor is it to say that Joe
Biden is an inauthentic expression of middle America. He really did
grow up in modest circumstances, he did not attend an Ivy League
school, and only Delaware's proximity to the nation's capital allowed
him to provide a more or less run-of-the-mill, upper-middle-class up-
bringing for his children.

In order to understand Biden's social position, one must think
about class less in terms of income and occupation and more in terms
of status and credentials. The senior senator from Delaware enjoyed
immunity from the press because he has held a prominent position in
our meritocratic society for more than thirty years. In the American
meritocracy, you earn status through achievement, and the way you
measure achievement may vary. The most common credential, of
course, is a college degree, the gravity of which is a function of the
school attended (community college, state school, liberal arts, or Ivy
League) and the level of education attained (associate's, bachelor's, master's, or doctorate). But there are plenty of other credentials, such as
wealth, celebrity, and taste.

In the political realm, mere survival is enough to earn distinction.
A long career in Washington establishes one's reputation as a party elder
and wise man. Frequent appearances on public affairs television shows
suggest that you are someone whose opinion matters. And an associa-

tion with the sites and accoutrements of fashionable opinion—the Council on Foreign Relations, the Alfalfa Society, the Democratic Party, the World Economic Forum at Davos, NPR, *Foreign Affairs* magazine, the *New York Times* op-ed page, and the latest trendy "big think" book on (a) the (always decrepit) state of American politics, economics, or culture, or (b) America's (always declining) place in the world—enhances the probability that your peers will consider you a "serious" person, no matter how unserious you may actually be.

Biden may have come from Scranton, but for most of his life he has been known more for congressional celebrity than the down-on-its-luck industrial city where he was born and raised. This makes sense. Ascension in the American meritocracy is a process through which an individual exchanges his small-town or suburban authenticity for big-city credibility. As the novelist E. L. Doctorow wrote in his 1980 *Nation* essay, "The Rise of Ronald Reagan," the fortieth president hailed from "such towns as Galesburg, Monmouth, and Dixon—just the sorts of places responsible for one of the raging themes of American literature, the soul-murdering complacency of our provinces, without which the careers of Edwin Arlington Robinson, Sherwood Anderson, Sinclair Lewis, and Willa Cather, to name just a few, would never have found glory. The best and brightest fled all our Galesburgs and Dixons, if they could, but the candidate [Reagan] was not among them." Like Doctorow's writers and other American meritocrats, Joe Biden left Scranton to pursue a larger purpose. It was not until the Obama campaign sought to establish its middle-class reputation that Biden's hometown became the top item on his résumé.

One weakness of a society organized around excellence is that there are always a whole lot more ordinary people than there are extraordinary ones. Biden's career may have accorded him respect from his fellow meritocrats, but such respect is often viewed with suspicion by the large numbers of Americans who do not subscribe to the regnant values in Los Angeles, San Francisco, or the East Coast megalopolis that stretches from Boston to D.C.

Thus, whenever Biden referenced the long-ago breakfast specials he enjoyed at a now-defunct greasy spoon, or mentioned his time spent loitering in hardware stores, he was distancing himself from his meritocratic standing and putting forward his democratic biography. Not everyone coauthors op-eds for the *Times* and takes weekly news quizzes proctored by David Gregory and George Stephanopoulos. But most everyone has ordered scrambled eggs and coffee at a local diner and shopped at one of the big-box stores that are strewn about the suburban landscape like confetti.

Palin was an interloper in meritocratic circles. Her critics viewed her degree in journalism from the University of Idaho as nothing special. She was a relative newcomer to state-level politics, and her state was thousands of miles away from the nation's power centers. She had never appeared on *Meet the Press*. She had never authored an important article. She spoke with a funny accent and unusual syntax. She was a pro-life conservative Republican, which in liberal eyes is about as uncool as you can get. And McCain had rewarded Palin's squareness by giving her the vice presidency, a job that in recent decades, Dan Quayle notwithstanding, has been reserved for either a presidential nominee's rivals or party fixtures with long Washington records.

What had Palin done, her critics asked, to deserve—to merit—the job? For whatever reason, the meritocrats did not recognize Palin's accomplishments (perhaps because those achievements hardly factored in the media coverage of her). They did not see her common-man appeal. They had no use, no respect, for the everyday hockey mom who took on the powers that be and came out on top.

Yet there was one Democrat who understood the ties that bound

Palin to a large swath of the American public. "I come from Arkansas," Bill Clinton said in September 2008. "I get why she's hot out there, why she's doing well. People look at her, and they say: 'All those kids. Something that happens in everybody's family. I'm glad she loves her daughter and she's not ashamed of her. Glad that girl's going around with her boyfriend. Glad they're going to get married . . . I like that little Down syndrome kid. One of them lives down the street. They're wonderful children. They're wonderful people. And I like the idea that this guy does those long-distance races. Stayed in the race for five hundred miles with a broken arm. My kind of guy.'"

Such sentiments were rare, however. The differences between Palin's biography and the typical meritocrat's drove the pundit class to distraction. For them, Palin's college experience was atypical and hence suspect. "She sure did attend the heck out of college," the movie critic Roger Ebert wrote in the September 11, 2008, *Chicago Sun-Times*. "Five different schools in six years. What was that about?" It was about having to work and study while balancing home, family, and ambition, but that must not count. Ebert was also puzzled that Palin wasn't a globetrotter as he was. "[H]ow can a politician her age never have gone to Europe?" he wrote. "My dad had died, my mom was working as a bookkeeper, and I had a job at the local newspaper when, at nineteen, I scraped together $240 for a charter flight to Europe . . . You don't need to be a pointy-headed elitist to travel abroad. You need curiosity and a hunger to see the world. What kind of a person (who has the money) arrives at the age of forty-four and has only been out of the country once, on an official tour to Iraq? Palin's travel record is that of a provincial."

Ebert was not only incorrect—by the time she was nominated, Palin had also traveled to Canada and Mexico—he was also extremely condescending. Two weeks with a backpack and a Eurail pass, or a semester spent partying—sorry, "studying abroad"—in Santiago de Chile on your parents' nickel are not the only ways to express "curiosity" and nonprovinciality. Trying absinthe in a Barcelona nightclub has little to do with the life of the mind. And yet world travel is an obsession for some Palin-haters, even though they never get around to specifying just how many times a person's passport ought to be stamped before he qualifies for high office.

"Is my heartfelt belief that travel broadens the mind and adds immeasurably to my understanding of the world a middle-class bit of snobbery?" Janet Street-Porter rhetorically asked in the *Independent* on September 14, 2008. "Do I sneer at Sarah Palin because she's happy at home in the featureless tundra of Alaska and doesn't feel the need to stare at the wonderful ceiling of the Sistine chapel, admire the Eiffel Tower, gasp at Ayers Rock, or be enchanted by the Taj Mahal?"

Yes.

What accounts for the off-putting mix of self-congratulation and disdain for others in Ebert's and Street-Porter's prose? One possibility is the frightening prospect of living under the rule of someone you believe has lesser status than you. This was a widespread reaction to the Palin nomination. She was identified as beneath writers like Ebert and Street-Porter because they believed she lacked the most important attribute in a meritocracy: brain power. In the meritocrat's eyes, international frequent flyer miles and a degree from the London School of Economics become metonyms for IQ. "She comes to us," author Sam Harris wrote in the September 29, 2008, *Newsweek,* "seeking the second-most important job in the world, without any intellectual training relevant to the challenges and responsibilities that await her." For Harris, a college degree, real-world work experience, a successful career in local and state politics, and common sense weren't enough.

No question, Sarah Palin's college trajectory was haphazard. When

Sarah Heath graduated high school in 1982, her plan had been to attend college in Alaska's sister state, Hawaii, where the weather would be warm and the sun would shine all year long. When Sarah and her friends got to the University of Hawaii at Hilo, however, they discovered that it rained all the time. They were miserable. So Sarah Heath transferred to Hawaii Pacific University, where she spent a semester. Turned out it wasn't the weather, it was the state that bothered her. Next stop was North Idaho College, in the state of her birth. She spent two semesters there, then transferred to the University of Idaho, where her brother was playing football. She also took classes at Matanuska-Susitna Community College in Palmer, Alaska, in the fall of 1985. She graduated from the University of Idaho with a degree in journalism in 1987.

College for Palin was about seeking her place in the overall scheme of things. She wanted to stay close to her friends, family, the Mat-Su Valley, and boyfriend Todd Palin, all while experiencing as much as she could of the wider world. Such a view of the college experience does not satisfy liberals, however. They expect political leaders to emerge from elite universities with a graduate degree and a heavily underlined copy of Fanon's *Wretched of the Earth* in hand. Liberals do this even though they routinely rank Harry Truman, who had no college education, among the greatest U.S. presidents.

As the actress Jamie Lee Curtis wrote in a September 3, 2008, entry on the *Huffington Post*, "When the call comes at 3 a.m. I want a mind who was at the top of their class, who has gravitas and a real intellect. I want a leader who is a scholar who can hold the history of civilization in his head and will read and learn from the past as he charts the future." In a September 16, 2008, *New York Times* column, David Brooks lamented that Palin "does not have a repertoire of historic patterns." The editor of *Newsweek,* Jon Meacham, asked in his magazine's October

13, 2008, issue: "Do we want leaders who *are* everyday folks, or do we want leaders who *understand* everyday folks?" Meacham clearly saw Palin as belonging to the former group, and he clearly preferred the company of the latter.

Palin's enemies went to extraordinary lengths to prove she was stupid. On October 9, Gawker Media editor in chief Nick Denton posted the image of a below-average report card under the headline, "Sarah Palin's High-School Grades?" "If the report card is a forgery, it's decent work," Denton concluded. "The grades are mediocre—appropriately the small-town girl scores a D in foreign language—but not so dreadful as to immediately stretch credulity." Denton should have taken another look. The documents, which also purported to show Palin's SAT scores, were a total fabrication. Anonymous bloggers had doctored them, using another blogger's score report as a template.

That did not prevent the images from appearing on the highly trafficked Web site Buzzfeed.com, where they received tens of thousands of views. "We can't be sure if it's real, but it's real embarrassing if so," the Web site's Scott Lamb wrote when he posted the item. "425 verbal? Ouch." But it was the dupes who had been suckered by this transparent fraud who really ought to have been embarrassed. On October 10, 2008, Wonkette posted the hoax under the headline: "Sarah Palin's Alleged SAT Scores Revealed!" "Actually a 425 verbal sounds about right," the blog's author pronounced. Predictably, the faux scores also showed up on the Daily Kos, where a blogger called them "credible" (the post has since been removed).

When two French Canadian comedians posing as French president Nicolas Sarkozy successfully prank-called Palin, they wound up as featured guests on the CBS *Early Show*. The fact that the Québécois had been able to play a fast one on the governor, who was polite and gracious in her conversation with them, was considered proof-positive that

Palin didn't know which way was up. Please. What was Palin supposed to do when an aide handed her a phone and said the president of France was on the line? Hang up? Ask for him to fax over his birth certificate before the conversation went any further?

Since they had no actual evidence that Palin was unintelligent, writers gussied up petty insults until the aspersions took on the appearance of serious arguments. Palin, Catherine Deveny wrote in the September 17, 2008, issue of Australia's *The Age,* is "a social experiment with lipstick." The GOP ticket comes across "like an old rich bloke with erectile dysfunction and his white trash trophy wife wearing glasses so she looks intellectual." Deveny wasn't about to stand for all this talk about the equal franchise, either: "[P]eople should have to pass an intelligence test before they're allowed to vote." The columnist Mary Mitchell wrote in the October 10, 2008, *Chicago Sun-Times,* "Sarah Palin makes me sick. She does. The potential elevation of Palin into the second-highest position in the country shows that we have finally sunk as low as we can go." Not true. In her columns, Mitchell proved we could sink much lower.

The critics of Palin's intelligence shared one thing in common: none of them had known, worked with, or even spoken to Palin. Interview the governor's supporters and critics in Alaska, however, and they will tell you that Palin is quite smart. And they should know. They are the people who have worked with her the closest, dealt with her the longest. "She's extremely intelligent in ways political professionals don't value," an Anchorage businessman who is critical of Palin told me. "Sarah is many things but she is NOT stupid," a longtime Alaska Republican and Palin critic wrote me in an e-mail. A senior campaign aide said, "She worked incredibly hard. Definitely a smart person." Her performance during the debate with Biden suggested as much.

When the haters went after Palin's smarts, they were attacking Tina

Fey's caricature of a political bimbo. Not the flesh-and-blood Sarah Palin. The caricature itself was a meritocrat's parody of the great, unwashed American majority. Self-professed intellectual superiority was the foundation for the Palinphobes' claim to rule. "The idea that you can join the PTA and wind up president sixteen years later is very disturbing to some people," speechwriter Lindsay Hayes said. "It's about what constitutes valid knowledge."

The American meritocratic elite places a high priority on verbal felicity and the attitudes, practices, and jargon that one picks up during graduate seminars in nonprofit management, government accounting, and the semiotics of Percy Shelley's "To a Skylark." Palin does not fit this mold, however. She speaks in a different patois. Her gut instinct and moral sense are what drive her, not trendy articles in the *New Yorker*. Rather than rely on the conventional wisdom, she listens, makes decisions, and then delegates authority to experts.

It is no fault of Sarah Palin's that today's liberal elites are wedded to a materialist, progressive, hyperintellectual world view that sees all phenomena as subject to rational control. Nor is Palin to blame for the left's refusal to acknowledge that there are other, equally valid ways of interpreting reality. The obstinacy is long-standing. "Today it is almost heresy to suggest that scientific knowledge is not the sum of all knowledge," Friedrich Hayek wrote in his 1945 essay "The Use of Knowledge in Society." "But a little reflection will show that there is beyond question a body of very important but unorganized knowledge which cannot possibly be called scientific in the sense of knowledge of general rules: the knowledge of the particular circumstances of time and place."

Hayek continued, "We need to remember only how much we have to learn in any occupation after we have completed our theoretical training, how big a part of our working life we spend learning particular jobs, and how valuable an asset in all walks of life is knowledge of people, of local conditions, and of special circumstances." This is the democratic well of experiential knowledge that sustains Sarah Palin. It is not easily measured by the SAT, the LSAT, the GRE, the GMAT, or the MCAT. But it is cognizance just the same. "It is a curious fact," Hayek wrote, "that this sort of knowledge should today be generally regarded with a kind of contempt and that anyone who by such knowledge gains advantage over somebody better equipped with theoretical or technical knowledge is thought to have acted almost disreputably."

Hayek died in 1992. He never met Sarah Palin. But he would have understood why some people despise her so.

POPULISM AND ELITISM

"Populism," Jeffrey Bell wrote in his 1992 book *Populism and Elitism,* "is optimism about people's ability to make decisions about their lives. Elitism is optimism about the decision-making ability of one or more elites, acting on behalf of other people. Populism implies pessimism about an elite's ability to make decisions for the people affected. Elitism implies pessimism about the people's ability to make decisions affecting themselves." This is the line on which most American political battles are fought.

Viewed through Bell's prism, George W. Bush was an unusual tribune of the masses. For starters, he was descended from the Connecticut WASP aristocracy. He embraced populism relatively late in his career. And his populist phase didn't last too long (from the 2002 elections to Hurricane Katrina), mainly because he ended up successfully uniting most of the country against him. Also, Bush's major second-term accomplishment, the Iraq surge—for which the nation continues to be in his debt—was an elitist policy, having been designed in a

Washington think tank and implemented over the objections of just about everybody.

What made Bush a populist was his obvious contempt for people who put on airs or thought that they were smarter than the rest of us. Liberal pointy-heads ground their teeth and repaid his ill will in kind. But they also made the mistake of expanding their circle of hatred to include all those who might have voted for Bush or reckoned he wasn't the lying, evil, anti-intellectual, Machiavellian Prince portrayed in the media. For instance, in a November 4, 2004, essay on Slate.com, the novelist Jane Smiley attributed Bush's reelection to the "[i]gnorance and bloodlust [that] have a long tradition in the United States, especially in the red states." Around the same time, the left-wing cartoonist Ted Rall wrote that "the biggest red-blue divide is intellectual." Such condescension and animosity characterized lefty polemic throughout the Bush presidency.

The late cultural critic Christopher Lasch identified the trend years before Bush arrived on the scene. "The new elites," he wrote in his 1995 book, *The Revolt of the Elites*, "are in revolt against 'Middle America,' as they imagine it: a nation technologically backward, politically reactionary, repressive in its sexual morality, middlebrow in its tastes, smug and complacent, dull and dowdy. Those who covet membership in the new aristocracy of brains tend to congregate on the coasts, turning their back on the heartland and cultivating ties with the international market in fast-moving money, glamour, fashion, and popular culture." In this passage, Lasch—who was no Republican—distilled the liberal attitude toward the American bourgeoisie. And yet if liberals viewed the blue blood George W. Bush as the embodiment of everything they felt was wrong with middle America, how would they react to Sarah Palin?

Class-based antagonisms may be rare in American politics, but Sarah Palin seems to be the exception that proves the rule. Her background, manners, and social status have been denigrated throughout her career. Her opponents routinely identify her with American redneck, hillbilly, "white trash" culture. Back in Alaska, former Alaska state senator Ben Stevens (son of former U.S. senator Ted Stevens) once referred to the folks who live in the Mat-Su Valley as "valley trash." Palin had the quote printed on a T-shirt and allowed herself to be photographed wearing it.

Little changed when Palin arrived in the Lower 48. Wonkette wrote that Wasilla was a "snowbilly trailer-trash burg." Andrew Sullivan called Palin's candidacy a "sputtering, ramshackle motorbike repaired in the backyard," and criticized what he called "Sarah Palin's cocktail waitress act." Catherine Deveny joked, "I'd love to see the White House lawn covered in cars up on blocks" if Palin won the vice presidency. And in her September 5, 2008, rant on the Canadian Broadcasting Corporation's Web site, Heather Mallick wrote that Palin "added nothing to the ticket that the Republicans didn't already have sewn up, the white trash vote, the demographic that sullies America's name inside and outside its borders yet has such a curious appeal for the right." Mallick continued: "White trash—not trailer trash, that's something different—is rural, loud, proudly unlettered (like Bush himself), suspicious of the urban, frankly disbelieving of the foreign, and a fan of the American cliché of authenticity."

This was foolishness. Yet Mallick did raise an important topic when she wrote of the supposed "white trash" tendency to be "proudly unlettered (like Bush himself)." Bush, after all, is a graduate of Yale and Harvard who reads books at a high clip. So what was Mallick talking about when she called him "proudly unlettered"?

The answer tells us a lot about the way Americans like to talk about class: by setting the mass of men against the "elites" who manage and represent the nation. The animosity is mutual. The elitist Mallick was referencing Bush's affect, his regular-guy manner: the homespun president with a Texas accent and cowboy hat who eats cheeseburgers, calls his chief adviser "Turd Blossom," and disregards pronunciamentos from the faculty lounge and Tom Friedman. Calling Bush "unlettered" was Mallick's way of saying that the president wanted nothing to do with the liberal intellectual elites who teach college; write newspapers, magazines, and books; and appear on cable news. It wasn't that Bush didn't read or think. It was that he didn't read the things Heather Mallick read, or think the things Heather Mallick thought. His heterodoxy was held against him.

To liberals, Bush at heart was a pretender, a man who pandered to the masses but was just another fortunate son. Most prominent populists, after all, are aristocrats with politics that diverge from those of their fellows. But Sarah Palin was an authentic representation of the American people—in all their strengths and in all their weaknesses and foibles. She lived far, far away from the Bush family retreat in Kennebunkport. She had not gone to an Ivy League school. The Christian tradition in which she was raised was even more exotic to liberals than Bush's Evangelical Methodism. She'd had many children (one of whom was a pregnant teen). Her husband belonged to a union. As mayor of Wasilla, Palin had actually officiated at a wedding held in a Wal-Mart. Nor did she run away from her background like the writers in E. L. Doctorow's essay. She embraced it, and she used her approachability to charm voters. A lot of folks couldn't resist. "What pulled people into those events was the idea that she wasn't an elite," Lindsay Hayes said. "They found in her a connection; she understood them."

There was always the danger that the connection could be severed. The October 22, 2008, Politico scoop that the Republican National

Committee had spent more than $150,000 on wardrobe for the Palin family was the only moment in the campaign when the governor's regular-folk street cred came into question. In her bombshell story, Jeanne Cummings reported that the RNC had authorized tens of thousands of dollars in expenditures at high-end outlets like Neiman Marcus, Saks Fifth Avenue, Barneys, Macy's, and Bloomingdale's. Pointing to the money the GOP spent on her clothes became a favorite tactic to deny Palin's authenticity.

The press made the clothes story into a big deal for absolutely no reason other than that it cut against Palin's image. In the seven days after Politico broke the news, the *New York Times* featured no fewer than twelve articles and columns mentioning Palin's wardrobe. The *Washington Post* contained eight different stories on Palin and clothes over the same week. Almost a year *after* the election, on August 12, 2009, the *Post* ran a story with the headline "Fate of Palin's Wardrobe Unknown," as though the clothes were the equivalent of Iraqi WMD. In an October 23, 2008 piece, *USA Today* writer Olivia Barker actually took time to interview "image experts" on the matter. "The total bill might make Joe Six-Pack spew his brew," Barker wrote. She quoted stylist Simon Doonan of Barneys, who said the RNC expenditure "doesn't seem frivolous to me," and blogger Amy Tara Koch, who said Palin "was a badly coiffed deer in the headlights" who "looked like she was straight out of a LensCrafters ad."

"I don't think Joe the Plumber wears Manolo Blahniks," Joy Behar crowed on the October 22 episode of *The View*.

It did not faze Palin's accusers that the story said absolutely nothing about her and a lot about the bizarre priorities of her handlers. "Voters turned on Sarah Palin not just because of her manifest unfitness for office," the *New York Times* columnist Frank Rich wrote in February 2009, "but because her claims of being a regular hockey mom were contradicted by her Evita shopping sprees," as though Palin was out behaving like a contestant on some sort of presidential *Shop Till You Drop.*

Palin, remember, had literally been taken from her job interview in Sedona to a hotel suite in Ohio to prepare for her debut, then to a hotel suite in the Twin Cities to prepare for her convention speech. She had no clothes with her other than what she had packed to visit McCain in Arizona in late August. Of course she and her family needed new threads for the campaign trail. Did they need these clothes at these prices? Absolutely not. The media was so obsessed with the numbers, however, that they rarely bothered to mention that Palin had neither authorized the purchases nor been aware of their costs. Nor is it actually clear where all the clothes *went.* Palin and her family wore many of them but not everything. When the clothes arrived, I'm told, Todd Palin looked at the price tag on one of his new belts and dropped it to the floor. *I'm not wearing that,* he said. The Palins were rightly offended by the idea that they had to "dress up" to be suitable for public consumption.

It was not only Palin's biography that made her the perfect vessel for populist politics. She also had experience in the field. Since her days on the Wasilla City Council, she had styled herself an advocate for the people in tension with the elites, whether those elites were Mayor Stein, Randy Ruedrich, Governor Murkowski, or the oil executives and lobbyists in Juneau. When she carried the populist colors to the national battlefield, however, she encountered a much more tenacious opponent: the media. They were unwilling to surrender their positions of authority. "[D]o I think that I am right," Jon Meacham wrote, "in saying that Palin's populist view of high office—hey, Vice President Six-Pack, what should we do about Pakistan?—is dangerous? You betcha."

The idea that Palin's populism was "dangerous" gained currency in

October 2008 when she drew attention to Barack Obama's relationship with the former domestic terrorist William Ayers. That relationship is well documented. On October 4, 2008, even the *New York Times* reported that Obama "has played down his contacts with Mr. Ayers." And while the *Times* also reported that the "two men do not appear to have been close," the paper did go on to note that Obama had served on two boards with Ayers, launched his first run for public office at "a coffee" in Ayers's house, and knew the ex-Weatherman-turned-professor as a friendly acquaintance from the Chicago neighborhood he called home.

Obama routinely minimized these contacts. Whenever he was confronted with this association, Obama called Ayers "a guy who lives in my neighborhood," "somebody who worked on education issues in Chicago that I know," and "somebody who engaged in detestable acts forty years ago, when I was eight."

Obama's evasion was telling. For him, the passage of time had diluted Ayers's misdeeds. In his eyes, abandoning bombing campaigns for radical educational theory had erased the stigma on Ayers and his wife and fellow Weatherman, Bernardine Dohrn. Their advanced degrees, writing, and teaching had turned them into respectable elites. To bring up their torrid history was impolitic. Impolite.

But the populist cannot forgive people like Ayers and Dohrn. The populist cannot comprehend why someone would treat with respect a couple who once condoned the murder of their fellow citizens. In populist eyes, no matter how many boards or foundations he sits on, no matter the fashionable causes to which he contributes, Ayers will always be a man who hated his country enough to support acts of violence against it. That is what Palin meant at the October campaign rally where she said that Obama was "someone who sees America, it seems, as being so imperfect, imperfect enough, that he's palling around with terrorists who would target their own country. This is not a man who sees America as you see America and as I see America." Palin's message was that Obama's politics and associations separated him from the bulk of Americans. That he was just another elite.

Palin's assertion that Obama was "palling around with terrorists" may have been an exaggeration. If so, however, it was exactly the sort of exaggeration that is commonplace during high-stakes political campaigns. And unlike a lot of campaign hokum, the phrase had a factual basis. Obama has never denied knowing or working with Ayers and Dohrn, both of whom were avowed members of a domestic terrorist group.

Rather than use Palin's salvo as the springboard for further reporting on the Ayers-Obama relationship, however, the pundit tribe went ahead and attacked . . . *Palin!* Campbell Brown said Palin's line was "just outrageous." Barbara Walters said such attacks were "smears." Bill Maher likened a Palin rally to a "hatefest." E. J. Dionne's October 15, 2008, column wondered, "Has John McCain, inadvertently perhaps, become the midwife of a new movement built around fear, xenophobia, racism, and anger?" Exhibit A was Palin's "palling around" line. "Ayers has been dragged into this campaign," Dionne wrote, "because there is a deep frustration on the right with Obama's enthusiasm for shutting down the culture wars of the 1960s." Not exactly. Ayers was a legitimate campaign issue because for years Obama hadn't had the good sense to run in the other direction whenever he came into view. What did that say about the Illinois senator's character?

The heated liberal reaction to the Ayers fusillade only confirmed its effectiveness. The media countered Palin by changing the subject, portraying her as a populist demagogue who was feeding the hatred of an unruly mob. On CNN, David Gergen said, "There is this free-floating sort of whipping-around anger that could really lead to some violence.

I think we're not far from that." The media trumpeted reports that spectators at McCain-Palin rallies shouted "Terrorist!" and "Kill him!"

"Sarah Palin is the Ensign Nellie Forbush," Andrew Greeley wrote in the October 15, 2008, *Chicago Sun-Times,* referring to a character from *South Pacific.* He meant that Palin is "an All-American girl as racist, this time a racist with her eye on the White House. She can stir up crowds to shout 'Kill him!' at the mention of the presidential candidate of the other party a couple of weeks before the national election." This was slander. Sarah Palin is no racist, and the Secret Service was never able to confirm that "Kill him!" had actually been said. As for the cries of "Terrorist!" those seem justifiable when one considers that Ayers *had literally been a member of a terrorist organization.* McCain-Palin rallies were filled with middle-aged and older suburbanites who brought along their love handles and small children. This is not what you'd call a frightening crowd.

The media blowback at Palin's stump speech was so intense, anonymous McCain sources felt compelled to inform the press that Palin had used the "palling" line without authorization. These anonymous gabbers were either ignorant or liars or maybe both. "The idea that she was going rogue with the 'palling' line was absurd," a senior McCain adviser told me. Sure enough, in their book *The Battle for America 2008,* reporters Dan Balz and Haynes Johnson disclosed an e-mail from Nicolle Wallace to Governor Palin that read: "Governor and Team: Rick [Davis], Steve [Schmidt], and I suggest the following attack from the *New York Times.* If you are comfortable, please deliver the attack as written. Please do not make any changes to the below without approval from Steve or myself because precision is crucial in our ability to introduce this." What followed were the lines that Palin delivered at the October 4 rally.

The e-mail reveals two things beyond the tactic's origin. It shows the snobbery and discomfort with which Schmidt and Wallace treated Palin. And it proves that the Alaska governor was a loyal soldier in an army that did not appreciate her true value.

THE PEOPLE'S PARTY

On October 18, 2008, Palin appeared on *Saturday Night Live*. It was her fourth and final trial of the campaign. Palin was walking right into the grizzly's cave.

It took guts to do the show. *SNL* had spoofed her mercilessly, and in many ways had defined her public image (negatively). Unsurprisingly, a huge audience tuned in—Nielsen loves Sarah Palin. In two skits—one in which she watched bemusedly offstage as Tina Fey performed her Palin impression, and in another where she danced along to Amy Poehler's "Moose Rap" on "Weekend Update"—Palin was a consummate performer. The viewers saw a politician at ease with the misfits who had made so much fun of her. She came across as comfortable, normal, and willing to poke a little fun at herself.

One of the kindest reviews came from the show's founder and executive producer, Lorne Michaels. "I think Palin will continue to be underestimated for a while," he told EW.com's Jennifer Armstrong after the show. "I watched the way she connected with people, and she's powerful. Her politics aren't my politics. But you can see that she's a very powerful, very disciplined, incredibly gracious woman. This was her first time out and she's had a huge impact. People connect to her."

The next day, as Barack Obama canvassed a neighborhood in Holland, Ohio, he encountered a man who identified himself as "Joe." While campaign embeds recorded the scene, Joe told the future president that he'd hoped to buy a small plumbing business soon. "Your new plan is going to tax me more, isn't it?" Joe asked. Obama, in full campaign mode, said no. Small businesses would get a tax credit to help defray health care costs, he said, and he had no plans to raise income taxes on families making less than $250,000 a year. Besides, Obama went on, higher taxes on the rich shouldn't scare people. "I think when you spread the wealth around, it's good for everybody," he said.

Obama's mini-debate with "Joe the Plumber" was notable in a few ways. First, in its unerring crusade to discredit anyone who stood in Obama's path to the presidency, the media subjected Joe to hostile and withering scrutiny. The press breathlessly related that (1) "Joe the Plumber"'s actual name was Samuel Wurzelbacher, (2) he would benefit from Obama's "middle-class tax cut," (3) he owed back taxes, and (4) he did not have a plumbing license. So what? None of that detracted from the key takeaway from Wurzelbacher's meeting with Obama: the future president was a tax raiser who forthrightly believed in wealth redistribution.

The inquest into Wurzelbacher's private life was so out of control that at one point an Ohio state government employee improperly authorized an underling to search for information on Wurzelbacher contained on state computer databases. Just as they had done to Palin, Obama's allies employed every possible means to discredit this bald, single, sometimes-out-of-work, thirty-something plumber.

Furthermore, the episode highlighted the continuing importance of the new media to presidential politics. As soon as Joe the Plumber ended his impromptu exchange with Obama, video of the encounter traveled across the globe via the Internet. Like with Palin, the Web-based media may have made Wurzelbacher famous, but it also expanded the ranks of his critics and enabled them to spread damaging information about him. Meanwhile, in its never-ending search for stunts and gimmicks, the McCain campaign embraced Wurzelbacher wholeheartedly. He appeared at McCain rallies, and Senator McCain mentioned him frequently during the final presidential debate. And all because the cameras had been rolling when Wurzelbacher asked his question. If they hadn't been, we would have never heard of Joe the Plumber.

Wurzelbacher's emergence coincided with Palin's controversial campaign oratory. By raising the issue of Bill Ayers, Palin had evoked the dissimilarities between the Americans who lived in trendy university enclaves and those who still lived in places where Ayers and Dohrn's past actions were unpardonable. Then Wurzelbacher arrived and added an economic component to Palin's cultural populism. In effect, he was saying that while the rich could survive Obama's tax hikes, and the poor might benefit from an increase in government transfers, the small-business-owning middle class would get the squeeze.

There was also an educational dimension to the populist critique. Wurzelbacher and his doppelgängers such as "Tito the Builder" were tradesmen opposed to the Obama coalition of highly educated professionals. For the anti-Obama plumbers, builders, and repairmen, liberal concerns over capping greenhouse gas emissions, higher taxes, and national health insurance were not policies to be supported on the basis of a theoretical ideal of "social justice." They were policies to be opposed because they would lead to a more intrusive government that would regulate, mandate, tax, and spend a working person's livelihood.

Hence, Palin and Wurzelbacher were leading an incipient revolt of the nonprofessional, rural, and religious against the coastal establishment. They represented the party of democracy: of local control, minimal government, and judicial constitutionalism. Obama, on the other hand, represented the party of technocracy: of rule by centralized elites, bureaucrats pushing and pulling the levers of the economy, and the judicial imposition of social change. What made Palin and Wurzelbacher seem threatening was that, unlike Bush and McCain, they had no connection whatsoever to the elites they opposed. Their actions exposed a rift in American politics and transformed the 2008 election from a partisan contest into a sociocultural one.

Bit by bit, they were moving the GOP out of the country club and turning it into the ordinary person's party.

The problem was that there was widespread confusion over who or what made up the "establishment." After all, from 2001 to 2007, the Republicans had controlled all three branches of government and maintained control over the executive and judiciary branches through 2009 (it's hard to tell sometimes, but as of this writing Democratic presidents have appointed only three of the sitting nine Supreme Court justices). Palin and Wurzelbacher were trying to mount a populist, insurgent campaign that, if successful, would benefit . . . the incumbent party. The ordinary people for whom they spoke did not think that made much sense. The country was willing to give the out-group power before it let the in-group have another shot at the wheel.

Moreover, voters had spent eight years living under the purportedly free-market and small-government conservatism of George W. Bush. In the face of the financial crisis, continuing Bush's economic policies (which had in fact expanded government and in many cases hindered the free market) made little sense to an electorate desperate to put Dubya behind it.

McCain, Palin, and Wurzelbacher came off sounding a little too much like William F. Buckley Jr. when he famously wrote that he'd rather be governed by the first two thousand names in the Boston telephone directory than by the two thousand faculty members of Harvard University. But Buckley said that at a time when conservative power in America was at an ebb, not at the apogee of Republican dominance inside the Beltway. Buckley wasn't antielitist; he was antiliberal-elitist. In 2008 Americans were disappointed with conservative elites. They wanted to trade for a new set.

By the time Colin Powell endorsed the Democratic ticket in October, Obama was well on his way to victory. Bush's unpopularity, the financial crisis, and John McCain's tepid relationship with the GOP core were all working to produce a good election night for the Democrats. On November 4, 2008, the American people chose Obama as their forty-fourth president. The election wasn't a landslide—Obama beat McCain 53 percent to 46 percent—but it was decisive. The Democrats gained seats in both the House and Senate, and Obama won every voting group except white men and women age thirty and up, rural voters, and white Evangelical Christians.

In hindsight, however, Palin's populism may have been not so much behind the times as it was slightly ahead of them. President Obama has ushered in a restoration of big-government liberalism, and the public is slowly becoming disenchanted with his agenda. It turns out that voters are not so keen on higher taxes, fees, energy prices, and deficits after all.

Palin is not afraid to criticize Obama. "Somebody's got to start asking President Obama questions" about how he plans to pay for his agenda, Palin said when I talked to her for a *Weekly Standard* article in the summer of 2009. In her July 3, 2009, resignation speech, she blasted "debt-ridden stimulus dollars," said that "today's Big Government spending" is "immoral and doesn't even make economic sense," and called the national debt "obscene." In a July 2009 interview with *Time* magazine, she called cap-and-trade "cap-and-tax," and said the policy would "drive the cost of consumer goods and cost of energy so extremely high that our nation is going to start exporting even more jobs to China."

I asked Palin about President Obama's response to the democratic upheaval in Iran. "Maybe they're tougher behind closed doors," she said. She noted that there were plenty of things "the most powerful man in the world" could do to help bring down Iranian president Mahmoud

Ahmadinejad, including a new round of international sanctions. She went after Obama's rhetoric. "It's not 'meddling' in another country's business when you understand that what happens over there affects us over here," she said. "I wish Obama was tougher in that area." Palin used her Twitter and Facebook accounts to communicate directly to her supporters. The medium—direct and casual—suited her.

The anti-big-government Tea Parties that sprang up around the country in the spring of 2009 were the first sign that the Obama agenda would encounter opposition. Then Obama's health care and cap-and-trade plans ran into hurdles in the summer of 2009. The left-wing and media reaction to the popular revolt against the new administration echoed treatment of Palin during the campaign. Rather than examine the reasoning and emotions behind the public's concern, the president and his allies in Congress and the media dismissed the opposition as crazy, misinformed, cynical, and artificial. For example, House Speaker Nancy Pelosi and majority leader Steny Hoyer wrote in *USA Today* on August 10, 2009, that "an ugly campaign is underway not merely to mispresent the health insurance reform legislation, but to disrupt public meetings and prevent members of Congress and constituents from conducting a civil dialogue. . . . Drowning out opposing views is simply un-American." In his August 20, 2009, column in *Time* magazine, Joe Klein wrote that opponents of Obamacare were "nihilist[s]" and "hypocrite[s]" exploiting "cynicism about government" in a "disinformation jihad" aimed at the "tight, white, extremist bubble" that is the conservative movement. Jimmy Carter said that opposition to the president was evidence of a "racist attitude." In his August 22, 2009, weekly address, the president himself said his opponents engaged in "willful misrepresentations and outright distortions" in order to "use fear to block change."

Barack Obama had the chance to temper populist disquiet. He had the opportunity to reorient American public policy in a moderate, bipartisan, and holistic way. He blew it. He opted for unreconstructed liberalism instead and demonized everyone who stood in his way.

The fight between the people and the elites rages on.

CHAPTER EIGHT
Sarah's Choice: What's Next for Palin and Her Party?

THE new populism had an unintended consequence. Because it seemed somewhat anachronistic, dissonant, anti-intellectual, and exclusionary, Palin's and Wurzelbacher's styles of antielitist politics shoved a whole lot of GOP intellectuals, Northeast Republicans, and moderates right into the Obama camp. A not-insubstantial portion of the Republican Party simply cleaved off from the conservative mountaintop, like a cliffside falling into the ocean. When Colin Powell endorsed Barack Obama on *Meet the Press* and said he didn't think Palin was ready to be president, Palin's center-right critics already included David Brooks, Peggy Noonan, Kathleen Parker, Christopher Buckley, David Frum, and Mike Murphy, among others.

These writers shared little culturally, economically, and, in many cases, politically with Palin and her supporters. They had every right to oppose the governor, but in so doing they provided cover for the machine-gun media's endless barrage on Palin's dignity. CNN correspondent Drew Griffin, for instance, was downright jaunty on October 21, 2008, when he informed Palin in an interview that "The *National Review* had a story saying that, you know, 'I can't tell if Sarah Palin is incompetent, stupid, unqualified, corrupt, or all of the above.'" Griffin did not understand that the quote had been taken out of context. Byron York, the article's author, was actually reporting on what other people had said about Palin, not registering his own opinion. But the distinction had made no impression on the CNN gang because the quotation appeared to confirm their preconceived views.

How any particular Republican felt about Sarah Palin said a lot about where he or she thought the party should go next. There were three chief reactions. For those who thought the GOP had lost its conservative moorings by embracing George W. Bush's big-government conservatism and foreign interventionism, Palin was just the sort of charismatic leader who could return the party to its origins. For those who thought the party was losing elections because its social conservatism and strident nationalism had alienated independent voters, however, Palin was kryptonite.

Mike Murphy told me his initial reaction to Palin was that the media would get excited about the first woman on a Republican ticket, then realize, "Oh, s**t! She's a Christian conservative!" This meant, Murphy went on, "of the next ten weeks, seven will be about Darwin." Murphy said he e-mailed Steve Schmidt as soon as Palin's nomination was announced. "This is a huge [expletive deleted] disaster," he wrote.

"Somehow we've confused base voters with swing voters," Murphy said. "A base voter would vote for a block of cement if it's a Republican." But the red meat that base voters gobble up also has a tendency to give swing voters acid reflux. And, indeed, as much as polling confirmed that Republican partisans loved Sarah Palin, the same numbers also showed that independent voters viewed her unfavorably. Palin mobilizes the troops, but that is no longer enough to win elections, as the Republican ranks have thinned to their lowest point in a quarter century.

The third reaction to Palin was to blame her for John McCain's defeat and to undermine her at every opportunity. Certainly a small set of McCain campaign operatives felt this way. And though it is impossible to know for sure who belonged to this group, as the McCain operatives conducted their guerrilla campaign against Palin using anonymous leaks to journalists, the infighting was intense. As Mark Shields put it, the recriminations began to resemble "a civil war in a leper colony. "

As the campaign drew to a close, McCain sources began calling Palin a "diva" and a "whack-job." The mainstream media allowed these ad hominem and inaccurate attacks to be made on background, with zero accountability for the individuals leveling the smears. "They were leaking anything they could that was damaging to Palin," a senior McCain adviser told me. "It undermined our ability to defend her when McCain sources were reinforcing the negative stereotypes."

The leaks got nastier once the election was over. A November 5 *Newsweek* "web exclusive, " for instance, included salacious details on the wardrobe expenditures and reported that "an angry aide characterized the shopping spree as 'Wasilla hillbillies looting Neiman Marcus from coast to coast,' and said the truth will eventually come out when the Republican Party audits its books." What insulting balderdash. Then Carl Cameron of Fox News reported that McCain sources had told him Palin (a) thought Africa was a country and (b) didn't know which nations were party to the NAFTA agreement.

Cameron must not have checked these claims with other sources in Palin's orbit, however, because if he had he would have learned, as I did, that the leakers had taken passing comments Palin had made in private and twisted her words in order to tar her reputation. A silly verbal misstep, a momentary reference to "the country of Africa" when she clearly meant "the continent of Africa," became "Palin doesn't know Africa is a continent." Of course she does. She was briefed extensively on the situations in African nations such as Zimbabwe and Sudan, and sources told me that they were even a little surprised by how much Palin already knew about the Sudanese government's proxy war on Darfur.

The NAFTA gaffe was even more absurd. Palin and her team were preparing for an interview with Spanish-language media. The hotel suite was noisy and crowded. The television was on. Policy and communications staff wandered in and out of the room. Palin's chief foreign policy aide, Steve Biegun, was walking the governor through some topics that were likely to surface in the interview: immigration, the Minutemen, remittances, amnesty, Hugo Chavez, Cuba, and so forth. He went through the various trade agreements: the North American Free Trade Agreement, the Central American Free Trade Agreement, the Colombia Free Trade Agreement, and the Panama Free Trade Agreement.

When Biegun finished, Palin said: *OK, Steve, one more time. Go from the top: who's in NAFTA, what are the key issues, etc.* That turned into "Palin didn't know who was in NAFTA." The assertion was almost laughable. Who did these people think Palin was? A fifth grader? Her state shares a huge border with Canada. How could she *not* be aware of the most important economic agreement between our two countries?

One should view the anti-Palin leaks as the opening salvos in the campaign for the 2012 Republican presidential nomination. In order to preserve their reputations—such as they were—John McCain's strategists did not want to be blamed for his loss. If that happened, nobody would hire them to work on the next campaign, which would be terrible for them. A lot of money is involved. So the aides made sure Palin took the blame instead. And since they knew they'd never work for Palin again, the leakers could simultaneously protect their image, bolster their buddy-buddy relationship with campaign reporters, and harm a future rival candidate by giving damaging information to a pliant press. The entire spectacle was embarrassing and without precedent. And it was totally undeserved. "Governor Palin never was critical of anybody personally on the campaign," the senior Palin aide told me. "Never, on her part, was there any exclusion of anybody among her advisers. She was without fail polite and loyal. Without fail."

The leakers' larger point was that Palin had hurt McCain. Was this true? The answer is no. She helped him. Yes, most voters did not think she was qualified to be president, and her unfavorable ratings were high. But look at this way: the McCain campaign received a jolt of enthusiasm and cash when it added Palin to the ticket. She rescued what was going to be a moribund and possibly divisive convention. And until the economy spun out of control in mid-September, it looked as though she and McCain might even pull off a royal upset. According to the national exit poll on Election Day, the people who said that Palin had been a factor in their vote backed McCain, 56 percent to 43 percent.

In the end, the McCain campaign ill served Sarah Palin. It made her famous but it also shoehorned her into a bad media strategy and a partisan straitjacket. Palin did the best she could and anonymous staffers repaid her by sliming her in the press. Everyone involved was relieved when the election was finally over. McCain returned to the Senate, his strategists returned to the insular world of political professionals, and Sarah Palin returned to Alaska.

As it turned out, though, the fun was just getting started.

You Can't Go Home Again

Palin's first year as governor had been remarkably successful because she worked with an ad hoc legislative coalition of Democrats and antiestablishment Republicans. That coalition broke down the moment Palin joined the Republican presidential ticket. Her forceful attacks on Barack Obama dispersed the bipartisan support she had accumulated over the years. The Democrats in the legislature defected en masse. And because she had unseated it, the GOP establishment never liked Palin and wanted her to go away.

Palin's celebrity did not expand her political capital in Juneau; it erased it. Beginning in November 2008, "People were confronted with policy differences with the governor," former Alaska state senator Gene Therriault said. "The call went out from the national Democratic Party to take her down. Some of the Democrats who worked with her previously took their marching orders." Gridlock ensued. Bipartisan comity was no more. Anybody who had the opportunity to score political points against Palin took a shot.

The Alaska Judicial Council, a body that recommends jurists to the governor, forced the pro-life Palin to appoint a pro-choice judge to the state supreme court. The legislature rejected Palin's choice for state attorney general. The governor and the legislature fought protracted battles over the replacement for Democratic state senator Kim Elton and over stimulus money from the federal government. Civility with the legislature became untenable. John Coale, the Washington, D.C.–based Democratic lawyer who set up Palin's political action committee and legal defense fund, told me, "Something had to change."

The problem wasn't so much Palin as it was Alaska. The political contours of the state were subtly shifting in an anti-Palin direction. The Obama campaign had several offices in Alaska before the Palin pick. The Obama campaign thought it had a chance in a rock-solid red state. Anchorage mayor Mark Begich just barely defeated Ted Stevens in the 2008 Senate race. Environmental concerns, historian Steve Haycox said, are driving Alaskan political change. Any development in Alaska generates a host of environmental impact statements, which have created a pocket industry of environmental consultants. They are not the sort of folks who vote Republican.

Furthermore, the real-world costs of global climate change are always in Alaska's headlines: polar bears, permafrost, the melting Arctic ice cap, and so on. The maturation of the conservation units that Congress created in 1980 means that there are lots of professional land managers in Alaska who are also unlikely to be Republican. The transience of the population has produced a surplus of young college-educated liberals moving to Alaska to work in the nonprofit sector. Moreover, the economic basis of Alaskan life is shifting. Prudhoe Bay oil production is down from its peak. The gas line may never be built. The energy industry is in relative decline, and without the energy industry, there's no Alaska. Or at least not the Alaska that the country has known for the last forty years.

Alaska tied Palin down in multiple ways. The state's distance from the rest of America made it difficult to travel to major cities (or small caucus and primary states) in the continental United States without a hefty time commitment and scheduling effort. After the 2008 election, every time Palin traveled outside Alaska, her enemies inside the state pilloried her for neglecting her job. This was a standard that applied neither to George W. Bush, who traveled the country campaigning for president while he was still Texas governor, nor to Barack Obama, who spent two of his four years as a U.S. senator running for president. Palin chafed at this inconsistency and still isn't used to the idea that a different standard applied to her.

Then there were the ethics complaints. Practically everything Palin did since she returned home was politicized by her enemies and, in some cases, criminalized. The moment she knew there would be trouble, Palin said, was when she returned to the governor's office in Juneau after the

November election. The gaggle of reporters assembled there asked her a few questions about the campaign. Palin answered them. Almost immediately, an ethics charge was filed against her for conducting political business from her state office. "That was part of the Democratic plan to grind her up," Gene Therriault said. "Use the ethics law as a blunt instrument to club the administration."

Palin's opponents filed close to two dozen ethics complaints against her. Meanwhile, according to the *Wall Street Journal,* Palin's office was inundated with 150 Freedom of Information Act (FOIA) requests for information regarding her schedule and contacts. Her staff spent most of its time as unwilling participants in a giant fishing expedition. "They knew how to file these," Palin told me. "They knew what category to file them under. We got the fake people, we got the people filing online."

The charges were frivolous. One complaint said Palin violated the law by mentioning her vice presidential candidacy on her state Web site. Another said that her wearing a T-shirt with the insignia of Todd Palin's sponsor in the Iron Dog snow-machine race constituted a conflict of interest. "It's a cold, outdoor event," Palin said. "I've been wearing Arctic Cat gear for many years. I wear a Carhartt coat and commercial fishing bibs, too." Yet another complaint was filed under the name of a character from a British soap opera. One suspected it was only a matter of time before someone complained on behalf of the turkey who was decapitated in the background as Palin gave a television interview around Thanksgiving 2008.

The state personnel board dismissed the complaints, one after the other. According to the governor, however, when one factored in all the wasted time and resources, the cost to Alaska amounted to some $2 million. "Why would I continue to put Alaskans through that?" Palin said. What's more, because state ethics law requires the accused to pay for her own defense, the Palins' personal legal bills added up to around

$500,000. The Palins aren't poor, but they aren't rich, either. Paying off the debt will take some effort.

Some of the charges were so silly that Palin wanted to pay the fines and move on. "I got to the point where I said, 'May I just plead guilty?'" she told me. But pleading guilty would have been political suicide. Palin's opponents in the legislature would have moved to impeach her on the flimsiest of pretexts. She had to fight it out, whether it was costing her money and peace of mind. "In politics you're either eating well or sleeping well," Palin said. "I want to be able to sleep well."

The accusations affected Palin emotionally. "Sarah's changed since the campaign," one prominent Alaska Republican told me. "She's much more nervous." Another said that Palin surrounded herself with a "victimization reward squad" that played to her sense of being wronged. A third said, "Since she's done the nomination thing, she's been off her game." A fourth associate told me that after the election, Palin made a habit of listening to talk radio, attempting to track what pundits were saying about her. Her Momma Grizzly instincts came out whenever her sons and daughters were mentioned. She could hardly give a speech in which she did not mention elite condescension and her ill treatment at the hands of Katie Couric and left-wing bloggers. Her public performances became personal testimonials to the damage the media can inflict on a person's reputation and career. Palin was right, of course. But these were arguments for polemicists to make, not statesmen.

Meanwhile, Palin's political operation was specializing in self-inflicted wounds. Palin ignored the legion of Republicans willing to move to Alaska and prepare her for a continued national presence. Her communications team rarely responded to inquiries from non-Alaskan journalists, even conservative ones. She canceled appearances at several major Republican and conservative events, including the Conservative Political Action Conference in February 2009; a speech to the GOP congressional campaign committees in June 2009; a planned August 2009 speech at the Reagan Presidential Library in Simi Valley, California; and another event that month at the Alaska Family Council in Anchorage. "They're endlessly smalltime," Mike Murphy said. "They're making it up as they go along."

This is how Palin has always operated, however. "On the big stuff," former adviser John Bitney told me, "her instincts are amazing. Stimulus, oil politics—she's very good. But she'll drive you nuts on the little stuff. Like scheduling. Trying to make an appointment with her. No time for political protocol. That's a large reason why her relationship with the legislature [was] so bad."

For Palin, the hostility directed at her was novel and shocking. "Everyone else in '08 had been in the game for decades," John Coale said. "They all had been there. This was somebody playing for the first time." Palin decided to fight back.

The turning point came in June 2009. On June 3, Palin introduced the conservative radio talk-show host Michael Reagan at a dinner in Anchorage. In her introduction, Palin clumsily paraphrased from articles by Newt Gingrich and author Craig Shirley. Palin attributed the statements to Gingrich and Shirley, but only once. Predictably, a left-wing blogger soon took to the *Huffington Post*—a virtual coffee klatch for Palin-haters—and claimed that the governor was guilty of plagiarism.

The charge did not go unanswered. Palin's lawyer issued a statement saying that the blogger's accusation was ridiculous, which it was, especially considering that *both* the current president and vice president are known to have lifted passages from other politicians in the past without any attribution whatsoever. Both Gingrich and Shirley said no plagiarism had occurred. The round went to Palin.

On June 8, the late-night comedian David Letterman made a partisan, crude, and unfunny joke involving baseball star Alex Rodriguez and Palin's underage daughter Willow. The former had "knocked up" the latter, Letterman said, on the Palins' recent trip to New York City. Palin had not watched the show when radio host John Ziegler asked for her reaction the next day. When Ziegler read the joke to her, Palin was taken aback. She called it disgusting. What happened next shocked her even more. "The reaction to my candid and heartfelt response blew me away," Palin said. "I all of a sudden became the bad guy. Who says I don't have the right to give a candid and heartfelt response? The reaction to it really opened my eyes: This is *ridiculous*. You're damned if you do and damned if you don't."

Palin demanded that Letterman apologize. She defended her position on the airwaves. Less than a week later, Letterman said the nasty crack had actually been directed at Palin's eighteen-year-old daughter, Bristol, as though that made it any less tasteless. Then Letterman admitted he'd been wrong to make the joke in the first place. Palin had won again.

In late June 2009, an Alaska Democratic blogger pasted the face of a pro-Palin radio talk-show host on the body of Palin's son Trig. The governor's camp released a withering statement, saying, "The mere idea of someone doctoring the photo of a special needs baby is appalling. To learn that two Alaskans did it is absolutely sickening . . . Babies and children are off limits." The blogger backtracked. She said she only had intended to ridicule the talk-show host, as though that made any difference.

"What if I hadn't responded?" Palin told me. "Well, then, the criticism would be, can't you stand up for the special needs community?" The constant bickering and shifting standards rankled her. "Well, enough is enough," she said. "I would like the opportunity to speak up and speak out."

The moment warranted a bold move. John Bitney said that in times like these Palin seeks spiritual and familial counsel. "Sarah Palin on a personal level is driven by spiritual guidance that has taken her to where she is today," he wrote in a July 2009 e-mail. "While she has learned to accept that guidance—she often alludes to it in her statements—she probably can't explain it fully," Bitney wrote. "And I am assuming that guidance is now apparently telling her it's time to heal herself, her family, and get grounded for whatever the future holds. I can tell you that I have learned to respect her guidance (wherever it comes from), for it has given her strength and direction to some unparalleled political heights."

Palin made a clear decision to defend her family's honor. "The toll on her family from all the events over the past three years has been extraordinary," John Bitney wrote in his e-mail to me. "She had a baby, Bristol had a baby, Track was sent overseas, and no doubt Piper and Willow have all the day-to-day issues that come from young women growing up." The parade of outrages against her and her children did not help. As 2008 turned into 2009, Palin got stuck in a trivial public spat with her daughter Bristol's ex-boyfriend, Levi Johnston, that only helped to fast-track his career as a reality television star.

Yet a politician's job is to serve her constituents, not to bicker with comedians and celebrity wannabes. Palin was caught in a trap. Her global celebrity was in tension with her duties to Alaska. Had she remained in office, the tension would have become more pronounced. Meanwhile, the agenda on which she had defeated Frank Murkowski had been enacted into law. One more year in office would have meant additional legal bills and constant juggling between the demands of family, work, and fame. The job had become demanding and unpleasant. "I can't fight for what's right when I'm shackled to the governor's seat," Palin said.

So she broke free.

SHOCK AND AWE

On July 3, 2009, in a speech delivered from her home on Lake Lucille in Wasilla, Palin told her constituents that not only would she not seek a second term, she would also be transferring authority to Lieutenant Governor Sean Parnell on July 26, abdicating her office with about eighteen months left to go. The announcement received global press coverage, dominated the weekend headlines, and gave stories about the late Michael Jackson a run for their money.

Palin was taken aback by the furies that her announcement unleashed. She heard some people say that the timing of her speech was odd. She disagreed. "Independence Day is so significant to me—it's sort of a way for me to illustrate that I want freedom for Alaskans to progress, and for me personally," she told me in our interview. Others said the motivation for her resignation was unclear. "I'm like, 'Holy Jeez, I spoke for twenty minutes'" giving reasons, she said. Bloggers conjectured that a horrible scandal was looming over her. Wrong again. Palin told me she'd even heard a rumor that she resigned because pornographic pictures of her were about to hit the Internet. "Between which pregnancies did I get to pose for those?" she said sarcastically. Hearing all the innuendo, Palin said to herself, "Really? You can't just believe what I'm saying?"

Palin's combativeness was pronounced. When she announced her resignation, the Internet rumor mill went into high gear. The left-wing blogs could not countenance the idea that the woman to whom they had devoted such enmity might actually be resigning for her stated reasons alone. There must be some other story, they wrote, some other snowshoe waiting to drop. The CNN anchor Rick Sanchez speculated on air that Palin might be pregnant. The Alaska blogger Shannyn Moore wrote on the *Huffington Post* that Palin resigned because she was "under federal investigation" for self-dealing in the construction of the recreation center in Wasilla. Other liberal bloggers parroted Moore's baseless accusations. Palin's team wasted no time in issuing a statement from the governor's lawyer that shot down Moore's blog. "We will be exploring legal options this week to address such defamation," the lawyer wrote. The FBI also came out and said Palin was not the subject of an investigation. Another malicious story batted down.

Palin said she had been thinking about her decision for a while and had talked to various people about it. In January, during her State of the State Address to the Alaska legislature, she asked lawmakers to put the previous year's election behind them. "I asked them not to allow those distractions that were on the periphery to hamper the state's progress," Palin said. But her plea went unheeded. "It became obvious in the last months especially that too many people weren't going to ignore those things on the periphery."

As the months passed, Palin arrived at the conclusion that she did not want a second term as Alaska's governor. She had achieved what she had set out to do. "I know that we've accomplished more in our two years in office than most governors could hope to accomplish in two terms," Palin said. "And that's because I hired the right people." For Palin to remain shuttling between Juneau, Anchorage, and Wasilla would waste both her and her constituents' time. And "I cannot waste time," she said. "I cannot waste resources."

"To her credit," Anchorage-based pollster David Dittman said, "she just didn't tip off a few people and go through the motions for a year and a half." Before the announcement, Palin gave no public sign that she was thinking of resigning. When I visited Alaska in May 2009, I heard widespread speculation that the governor would not run for reelection, but no one mentioned the possibility that she would resign. That announcement, Dittman said, was "out of the blue." Alaska's next governor, Sean Parnell, reportedly found out that he was getting a promotion only a few days prior to Palin's announcement. Randy Ruedrich also expressed surprise. And when I asked another plugged-in Alaska Republican for comment on Palin's decision, the response via e-mail was, "Where do I begin?"

Not everyone was surprised, however. "The reality is, this was in the works for a long time," John Ziegler, who is as close to Palin as anybody in the media, told me. "The evidence is overwhelming." Ziegler pointed to her June 2009 speech introducing Michael Reagan, where Palin used the phrase, "If I die, I die," in reference to her political future. She would repeat those words after she announced her resignation. In an interview that Palin did with *Today* at the height of the Letterman controversy, Palin said, "I don't need a title to effect change." And in a June 9 interview, when Ziegler asked Palin if she had thought about resigning, Palin said yes.

"She was clearly trying to let everybody know this," Ziegler said. But the message did not get through. And the public was left shocked and confused.

THE NEXT CHAPTER

Palin is right when she says that she does not need "a title to effect change." On the campaign trail she discovered a power greater than public office: the power of celebrity. For better and worse, she enjoys the type of fame most politicians can only dream of. Her every move is showcased on television screens and featured in *People* magazine. Her every utterance shapes the contours of public debate.

For example, take Palin's claim that President Obama's health proposals could lead the government to establish "death panels" that would determine the age or conditions at which the government would no longer pay for medical care. On August 7, 2009, Palin posted the following message on her Facebook page:

> The Democrats promise that a government health care system will reduce the cost of health care, but as the economist Thomas Sowell has pointed out, government health care will not reduce the cost; it will simply refuse to pay the cost. And who will suffer the most when they ration care? The sick, the elderly, and the disabled, of course. The America I know and love is not one in which my parents or my baby with Down syndrome will have to stand in front of Obama's "death panel" so his bureaucrats can decide, based on a subjective judgment of their 'level of productivity in society,' whether they are worthy of health care. Such a system is downright evil.

Palin's visceral and evocative phrasing captured the public imagination and provoked a harsh reaction from liberals. In her August 9, 2009, *New York Times* column, Maureen Dowd wrote that Palin was "downright crazy" and had become "unhinged by fame"—before Dowd repeated a scurrilous rumor that the Palins were about to divorce. On August 14 in the *Times,* Paul Krugman wrote that Palin's speculative argument was a "complete fabrication." In an August 18, 2009, column in the *Washington Post,* Richard Cohen likened Palin to Joe McCarthy and wrote that to suggest a death panel "exists is reprehensible. To state it outright is either boldly demagogic or just plain loopy." By August 22, Palin's argument warranted a presidential response. "As every credible person who has looked into it has said, there are no so-called death panels—an offensive notion to me and to the American people," Obama said in his weekly radio address. "These are phony claims meant to divide us."

Let's stipulate that the health care proposals circulating on Capitol Hill in the summer and fall of 2009 did not explicitly authorize a "death panel." That would be absurd. But that is also not what Palin was arguing. What Palin was saying was that the only way a national health care system can control costs is by denying treatments, and that the people most likely to be denied treatments in such a system are the old and infirm.

This is not a "loopy" idea. In an April 2009 interview with David Leonhardt in the *New York Times Magazine,* it was none other than President Obama who said that while he had been ready to pay for his dying grandmother's hip-replacement surgery himself, "Whether, sort of in the aggregate, society making those decisions to give my grandmother, or everybody else's aging grandparents or parents, a hip replacement when they're terminally ill is a sustainable model, is a very difficult question. . . . I mean, the chronically ill and those toward the end of their lives are accounting for potentially 80 percent of the total health care bill out there."

Leonhardt asked Obama how society should "deal with it."

"Well," Obama said, "I think that there is going to have to be a conversation that is guided by doctors, scientists, ethicists. And then there is going to have to be a very difficult democratic conversation that takes place. It is very difficult to imagine the country making those decisions just through the normal political channels. And that's part of why you have to have some independent group that can give you a guidance."

A panel, if you will.

When Obama raised the specter of government rationing, the press treated the matter evenhandedly. On April 30, 2009, Peter Baker wrote in the *New York Times*:

As an intellectual matter, it's one thing to say that it makes no sense for a country to spend so much on procedures that ultimately will do little to extend or improve the lives of those nearing death. But as a personal matter, it's another to deny your own grandmother an operation that may at least make her last days more comfortable. Some conservatives have cited Mr. Obama's story to make the case that his plan to expand access to health care and reduce costs ultimately will result in rationing, of the kind that might have denied his grandmother the surgery unless she paid the bill on her own.

Things were different when Palin brought up rationing, however. In an August 14, 2009, article headlined "False 'Death Panel' Rumor Has Some Familiar Roots," the *New York Times* reporters Jim Rutenberg and Jackie Calmes mentioned neither the David Leonhardt interview with Obama nor the controversial writings of White House adviser Ezekiel Emanuel, which explicitly deal with "Principles for allocation of scarce medical interventions"—i.e., rationing. Instead the reporters dismissed Palin's argument altogether, equating it with the "modern-day viral Internet campaigns that dogged Mr. Obama last year, falsely calling him a Muslim and questioning his nationality."

This was incorrect. The accusation that Obama is a Muslim has no basis in fact. Palin's evocation of the "death panel," on the other hand, is an extrapolation based on her analysis of the Democrats' health care proposals. Rutenberg and Calmes's statement that "[t]here is nothing in any of the legislative proposals that would call for the creation of death panels or any other governmental body that would cut off care for the critically ill as a cost-cutting measure" misses the point; Palin was writing about the *unintended* consequences of the legislation. As she noted in subsequent written testimony submitted to the New York

State Senate Aging Committee on September 8, 2009, "The fact is that any group of government bureaucrats that makes decisions affecting life or death is essentially a 'death panel.'" According to Palin, to the degree that Obamacare empowers government regulators, bureaucracies, and the unelected Independent Medicare Advisory Council, it lays the foundation for a dystopian future.

In a subsequent Facebook message, Palin targeted Section 1233 of the House Democrats' health care reform bill, which authorized Medicare reimbursements to physicians who consulted with seniors on advanced directives and end-of-life counseling every five years or "if there is a significant change in the health condition of the individual." On August 12, 2009, Palin wrote:

> Now put this in context. These consultations are authorized whenever a Medicare recipient's health changes significantly or when they enter a nursing home, and they are part of a bill whose stated purpose is "to reduce the growth in health care spending." Is it any wonder that senior citizens might view such consultations as attempts to convince them to help reduce health care costs by accepting minimal end-of-life care?

Again, liberals freaked out at Palin's characterization. In a town hall meeting in Portsmouth, New Hampshire, that week, President Obama said that Palin's criticism was one of many "wild misrepresentations that bear no resemblance" to what's in the bill. But then Obama explained the controversy to the audience in a manner that suggested that Palin wasn't so off the mark after all. "[I]t turns out that I guess this arose out of a provision in one of the House bills that allowed Medicare to reimburse people for consultations about end-of-life care," Obama said. Exactly. Palin was concerned that such reimbursements might give rise to perverse incentives for doctors to emphasize the high cost of palliative care.

At the town hall, Obama said that "right now insurance companies are rationing care." "So why is it," Obama asked the town hall participants, "that people would prefer having insurance companies make those decisions rather than medical experts and doctors figuring out, you know, what are good deals for care?"

For Obama, there is no difference between rationing by price—being unable to purchase a good because one cannot afford it—and rationing by fiat—i.e., having the government tell you what you can and cannot buy. In a market system, you can always buy another insurance plan; the problem with American health care today is that the market is broken. There are fifty state markets for health insurance, not one national market; each of the fifty markets is heavily regulated with state government mandates that increase prices; the federal government uses its monopsony power to bid down the price of the medical services it purchases and thereby raises costs for everyone else. And yet the reason that a majority of people opposed Obamacare in the late summer of 2009 was that America's hybrid system of government and private insurance still offered many different choices and avenues for redress. In a government-dominated system, however, there are no alternatives to fiat rationing. What bothered people about Obamacare was the sense that it would remove individuals from making their own decisions on sensitive and important matters such as advanced directives and end-of-life care. That is why the "death panel" phrase had such impact. Obama did not understand this, because he is beholden to a technocratic view of politics that stipulates that the "experts" know best, whether the public likes it or not.

The controversy over the "death panel" led to a paradox. Even as Obama, Democrats, and the media said that Palin was spreading "rumors" and "fabrication[s]," the bipartisan leadership of the Senate Finance Committee announced that nothing resembling Section 1233 would appear in their health care bill. So the end-of-life counseling component of the death panel was dead—even though liberals said it had never existed in the first place.

The bottom line was that with just a few Facebook messages, Sarah Palin had done more to influence the debate over health care than just about any other Republican politician.

As a celebrity, Palin exerts a tremendous hold over the people she encounters. I've witnessed her ability to wow a crowd twice, at the Republican convention in August 2008 and again in April 2009, at the annual Vanderburgh County Right to Life Dinner in Evansville, Indiana. Palin gave the keynote speech. The audience was captivated.

Before the dinner, a volunteer named Bob took me to an auditorium where the chairman of the Republican National Committee, Michael Steele, was going to answer questions. I asked Bob what he thought about Sarah Palin. He liked her. "I'm an old guy," he said. "But we need to get people who stand for something."

A while later, when Sarah and Todd Palin entered the large hall where the dinner was being held, a huge crowd of well-wishers surged toward the couple. Normally buttoned-down pro-life activists squealed at Palin, trying to get her attention, trying to capture a piece of her celebrity. "Sarah!" they shouted, as they waved and smiled at her. "Over here!"

No one seemed to be bothered by Palin's remarks. "They're going to crucify me if I say yes to traveling outside the state of Alaska," she said of her opponents in the Alaska legislature. She read aloud a list of factoids about her state. "If I'm wrong on any of this trivia, I don't want Katie Couric calling me," she joked. She took on Obama's stimulus bill, saying that it would only add to the federal deficit. Americans can't be "enslaved to these nations that hold our notes," she said. The standing-room-only audience loved every minute.

The next morning, April 17, Palin went to the local Biaggi's franchise (an Italian restaurant chain popular in the Great Lakes States) to meet with local members of S.M.I.L.E. on Down syndrome. The cameras snapped as the Palins entered the dining room and greeted the attendees. Then those of us in the press were asked to leave out of respect for the families' privacy.

Palin demonstrated a true commitment to the families she met that day. "Having a child with Down syndrome brings with it a multitude of questions and concerns," Nina Fuller, S.M.I.L.E. on Down syndrome's executive director, wrote me in an e-mail. "It is always encouraging to learn from other parents who have traveled the road and are at least a mile or so down the path. S.M.I.L.E. stands for Support-Management-Information-Love-and-Encouragement. That is our goal in meeting with the Palins—to provide these [things] to another family with a little guy with Down syndrome."

As I left Biaggi's, I kept thinking of Bill McKeon, a bald, bespectacled older gentleman who had attended the dinner the night before. McKeon, who played for the Evansville Braves back in 1956, had made sure that a group of reporters understood just how much he liked Sarah Palin. "She's a strong-headed woman," McKeon said. "She's for the people. Sarah is the Joan of Arc of the twenty-first century, here to lead us, Republican, Democrat, conservative people."

Someone asked McKeon if he'd vote for Palin for president.

"A hundred times," he said.

When Palin announced her resignation, the conventional wisdom immediately gelled behind the position that she could no longer win the GOP presidential nomination in 2012. Yet the reality is more complicated. Palin's supporters viewed her decision not to seek reelection sympathetically. A Gallup poll released on July 7, 2009, recorded that 67 percent of Republicans wanted Palin to have a role as a national political figure. A Rasmussen poll from July 2009 found that Mitt Romney, Palin, and Mike Huckabee were in a statistical tie for the Republican nomination. When you expand the pool to include all voters, however, Palin faces a much tougher challenge.

One lesson from Barack Obama's candidacy is that a politician should seize his (or her) moment. Elite opinion, remember, thought that Barack Obama wasn't ready to run for president in 2008. He should sit back, the argument went. Gain seasoning. Master a few issues. Wait for his turn. But Obama understood that when you do that, you end up being Richard Lugar. Obama understood that once the spotlight is on you, it's foolish to let it pass on to someone else. He ignored the naysayers. He launched his campaign. Now he lives at 1600 Pennsylvania Avenue.

Ronald Reagan's late campaign manager John Sears had a term to describe what voters look for in a presidential candidate. The term was "appropriateness." Sears meant that John Q. Public wants to support the guy who best fits his mental picture of what a president should be. Does Palin have such "appropriateness"? The verdict is mixed. Certainly there's a latent hunger for a viable female presidential candidate who isn't Hillary Clinton. What's more, Palin looked authentic and commanding in her speech to the 2008 Republican National Convention. She performed ably in the vice presidential debate.

Throughout her career, Palin has seemed most "appropriate" at those moments when she sensed that the populace was diverging from the political class that ruled over it. Palin would exploit that split and win office as the people's spokesman. That is what happened when she saw that Wasillans were tired of the non-ideological, nonpartisan, unexciting mayoralty of John Stein; when she saw self-dealing among

Republican insiders in Anchorage and Juneau; when she saw that Alaskans were tired of Frank Murkowski and the lobbyist culture he nursed and protected. That is what she and John McCain tried to do in 2008, when Americans had grown tired of George W. Bush and Republican misrule.

The next time Palin sees a gap separating the people and their government, she may try to jump in and fill it. "I think she believes she has a mission," David Dittman said. "And I agree with her. She feels she has a duty, a mission, a purpose in life. And all that other stuff is secondary."

It has taken all that sense of purpose and inner strength to survive the recent trials. In the past couple of years, Sarah Palin has given birth at forty-four years old, to a special needs child; learned that her seventeen-year-old daughter was pregnant; been placed on the GOP presidential ticket; seen her nineteen-year-old son deployed to Iraq; spent two grueling months on the campaign trail; had her personal e-mail hacked; dealt with harsh and unfair media coverage; lost an election; returned to find that her enemies had made it impossible for her to do her job; and listened as a late-night talk-show host made cruel sexual jokes about her fourteen-year-old daughter.

Neither Palin nor the people who love and hate her are going away. "It's not retreat," Palin told me after she resigned. "It's moving more aggressively than ever to fight for what's right." Today the Palinistas and Palinphobes are as much a part of the national scene as they have been part of Alaska's. Since her debut, Palin has sparked curiosity and revulsion, devotion and ill will, admiration and scorn, in equal measure. For whatever reason, the press cannot take its unblinking eye off her. To the media and her detractors, she is a force of nature. She cannot be ignored.

"She's imprisoned them," one Anchorage businessman told me. "By controlling their minds. They are obsessed with her. They can't think beyond her. They are constantly yammering about how stupid she is, which is a constant Democratic error, because they always assume their opponents are stupid, so they underestimate them and get their butts kicked."

Sarah Palin is routinely underestimated because the media portrayal of her is grossly inaccurate. The media have reached the point of parody in their political coverage, and Palin exposes much of the absurdity. Today's media construct narratives about public figures that bear little relation to reality and yet are impervious to facts. The storyline that "Palin is stupid" or "Palin is a Luddite" is on par with the story that "Al Gore is an intellectual" (he was an average student at Harvard) or "George W. Bush is a religious zealot" (he is not) or "heart surgery changed Dick Cheney into a radical" (a bizarre idea). For today's media, things must be black and white. Palin has to be dangerous, Gore has to be smart, Bush has to be driven by his faith, and Cheney has to be a threat to his country. To argue otherwise would be to damage the warped and distorted lens through which the media view the world. To argue otherwise would be to question the absurd caricatures the partisan media concoct in the service of their larger goal—an antinationalist, anticapitalist, antitraditionalist agenda. To argue otherwise would be to challenge the media's self-proclaimed authority. And that is forbidden.

The story of Sarah Palin is the story of American political journalism's intellectual bankruptcy.

And yet Democrats and the media have been unable to dull Sarah Palin's spirit. When she resigned her office at a picnic in Fairbanks on July 26, 2009, Palin brimmed with confidence and purpose. "Let's all enjoy the ride," she said to the crowd. Her supporters stood in thrall to the woman from Wasilla. As she walked the picnic grounds, serving hot dogs and shaking hands, she was mobbed by people trying to connect with this misunderstood populist from the North. Old folks took pictures. Children asked for autographs. And from all directions, over the din of the critics, she could hear the voice of the crowd . . . calling her name.

ACKNOWLEDGMENTS

The author extends his gratitude and appreciation to Glen Hartley and Lynn Chu at Writers Representatives; Adrian Zackheim and David Moldawer at Penguin Sentinel; Bill Kristol, Fred Barnes, Richard Starr, and Claudia Anderson at the *Weekly Standard*; John McCormack, Thomas Johnson, and Kevin Vance for research assistance; Gerard Alexander, Sonny Bunch, Ross Douthat, Yuval Levin, and Robert Messenger for reading the manuscript; John Farley and Tom Phillips for their forbearance; and Jim Muller, Stephen Haycox, the Forty-Ninth State Fellows, Dave and Jean Bundy, and everyone else who made him feel so welcome during his visit to Alaska.